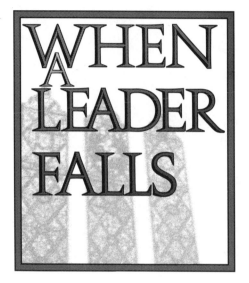

WHEN A LEADER FALLS

WHEN A LEADER FALLS

WHAT HAPPENS to EVERYONE ELSE?

JAN WINEBRENNER & DEBRA FRAZIER

BETHANY HOUSE PUBLISHERS
MINNEAPOLIS, MINNESOTA 55438
A Division of Bethany Fellowship, Inc.

Published by Bethany House Publishers
A Ministry of Bethany Fellowship, Inc.
11300 Hampshire Avenue South, Minneapolis, Minnesota 55438

Printed in the United States of America

Library of Congress Cataloging-in-Publication Data

Winebrenner, Jan.
When a leader falls / Jan Winebrenner, Debra Frazier.
         p. cm.

     1. Clergy—Sexual behavior. 2. Clergy—Family relationships. 3. Clergy—Professional ethics. 4. Clergy—Pastoral counseling of.   5. Spouses of clergy—Pastoral counseling of. I. Frazier, Debra. II. Title.
BV4392.W56   1994
174'.1—dc20   93-45529
ISBN 1–55661–335–0   CIP

With special thanks
to our parents and
our husbands
for their commitment to faith
and fidelity.

Our deep appreciation to

Beverly and Andrea,
Ted and Ryan,

and all those who shared their stories with us,
with the prayer that the Body of Christ
would be strengthened.

DEBRA FRAZIER is a free-lance writer and an instructor in English/writing at Richland Community College. She is the co-director of the Southwest Christian Writers Conference. Debra and her husband Dan have had over twenty foster children in their home, eventually adopting four of those children. They make their home in Texas.

JAN WINEBRENNER is a free-lance writer and author of four books. She is the founder of the Prestonwood Christian Writers Guild and co-founder/director of the Southwest Christian Writers Conference. She and her husband have two children and make their home in Texas.

Contents

Introduction: The Sin Against the Body 9

Part 1: Voices
1. Voices From the Bottom of the Heap 23
2. A Forever Tragedy 35
3. A Parishioner's Story..................... 59
4. Voices of Leadership...................... 77
5. A Little Bit of Leaven 93

Part 2: Choices
6. Choices From the Bottom of the Heap..... 113
7. And Jill Came Tumbling After 131
8. How Could We Not Know?................. 143
9. The Question of Confrontation 157
10. Working Through the Aftermath 173
11. Lives That Can Be Observed............... 193
Recommended Reading....................... 207

Introduction

The Sin Against the Body

"I can't believe this! It's been more than a year—I thought I was over it!"

The man speaking shook his head and turned to a colleague seated on his left. "This is unbelievable!" he exclaimed.

A small group of Christians had gathered to discuss the topic of moral failure among Christian leaders. Among them were writers, counselors, editors, publishers, and pastors.

Several months earlier, Ted Morris, a senior pastor, had discovered that three members of his staff had been guilty of sexual misconduct. Along with his associate minister, Ryan Pollard, he had overseen the discipline and restoration (to the body, not to the ministry) of the guilty members. They had led the church in decision-making, offering private counseling for each of the betrayed spouses and providing loving care for the family members. They had implemented a generous financial plan to ensure that the innocent parties would not suffer further misery and humiliation. They had walked through the tragedy with more wisdom, love, and sensitivity than most church leaders. They had seen the matter through with kindness and a thoroughness that should have allowed them, a year later, to be able to say, "There, that's done. Now, let's move on to other things."

And they *had* moved on to other things. Once the restoration process was implemented, both men had taken a brief sabbatical to recover from emotional and spiritual exhaustion. Then they had returned to their tasks, shifting their focus off their grief and back on to the regular ministries of their church. Now, one year later, the congregation was thriving, membership was up, and the mood of the church was enthusiastic. It appeared they had put the moral failure behind them. But that day, as the memories returned, Ted discovered that emotions he believed were disarmed remained hot to the touch.

At one point during the conversation, he slammed his fist against his forehead, as if doing so would somehow displace the emotional and spiritual pain of the whole sordid mess. But the pain wouldn't go away. Not for Ted. Nor for Ryan. Nor for the publisher. Nor the editor. They had all known the individuals involved in the scandal. They all continued to grieve. And to suffer. And to question.

Weeks may pass, even months and years, but the pain inflicted when a Christian leader falls is a stubborn pain. Sometimes throbbing, sometimes a dull ache, it is present and persistent, regardless of the amount of time that has elapsed.

Why? What is it about sexual sin that makes it different from other sins? Why is adultery within the church so painful and destructive? Why is it that a man or woman in leadership can gossip and the church does not reel? Why is it that a leader can commit any number of sins in a day—hypocrisy, poor stewardship, lack of compassion—and though the body may sway a bit, even stagger, it continues to stand? But let that man or woman become involved in sexual promiscuity and the body trembles; sometimes it topples to the ground in agony, and its voice is choked by the dust churned up by its fall.

(Because immorality is a growing problem within the body of Christ, it is likely—probable—that someone reading this may have been the *cause* of such trauma in a congregation. If so, you are already feeling the burden of guilt and shame. But before you close these pages and run for shelter, please understand that we are committed to the healing of the *whole* body, including you. It is our prayer that a clear, biblical understanding of what has happened will make repentence, forgiveness, and restoration a joyous reality in your life.)

It is obvious, isn't it, that sexual sin within the church has different consequences than other sins. Those of us who love God and His church have observed this, but we don't understand it. We're not sure why it's true.

The apostle Paul's letters give us insight that helps to explain: "Do you not know that your bodies are members of Christ himself? Shall I then take the members of Christ and unite them with a prostitute? Never! Do you not know that he who unites himself with a prostitute is one with her in body? For it is said, 'The two shall become one flesh.' But he who unites himself with the Lord is one with him in spirit. Flee from sexual immorality. All other sins a man commits are outside his body, but he who sins sexually sins against his own body" (1 Corinthians 6:15–18).

Strong language—and a *strong* metaphor. United with a prostitute? Before we cringe and shrink away from this awful picture of sexual sin, let's allow Paul to show us why this imagery is so appropriate.

"The body is a unit, though it is made up of many parts; and though all its parts are many, they form one body. So it is with Christ. For we were all baptized by one Spirit into one body—whether Jews, Greeks, slave or free—and we were all given the one Spirit to drink. Now the body is not made up of one part but of many. . . . Now you are the body of Christ, and each one of you is a part of it" (1 Corinthians 12:12–14, 27).

Now we begin to understand: As Christians, our bodies are a part of Christ's own body. And we can't escape the meaning here: When we engage in sexual promiscuity we join Christ with the prostitute. We link the holy Son of God with a harlot.

Paul continued by saying that sexual sin, unlike other sins, is "against the body," against our own flesh. Not only do we defile Christ's body, but we also defile our own flesh.

In vivid language, *Matthew Henry's Commentary on the Whole Bible* describes the awfulness of sexual sin in terms of "uncleanness" and "pollution." The style of more contemporary commentaries seems weaker than that of Mr. Henry, who writes, "He [the Christian] casts vile reproach on what his Redeemer has dignified to the last degree by taking it into union with Himself."[1]

---

[1]Matthew Henry, *Matthew Henry's Commentary on the Whole Bible* (Grand Rapids: Zondervan, 1961), p. 1812.

Don't miss the beauty of this last phrase: *Christ has taken us into union with himself.* He has dignified our bodies through the promise of resurrection and the act of redemption. Our bodies are not to be abused by promiscuous sexual behavior. The body *matters.* What is done by the body, to the body, through the body, has great significance. Because of the resurrection. And because of redemption.

There's more, Paul says: "You are bought with a price." Body, soul, and spirit are God's. Our flesh is Christ's, and we have no right to unite what is His with that which He abhors. We have no right to use for our own pleasure that which He purchased at such a high price—His own blood. We can't ignore this magnificent truth. God places great value on our individual bodies.

But the consequences of sexual sin grow still greater and more far reaching when we look at Paul's discussion of the church. Throughout the New Testament, but especially in the apostle Paul's writings, we see over and over again the teaching that the individual Christian is united with all other Christians to comprise a larger body, the body of Christ.

In his book *The Body*, Charles Colson reminds us of the ancient creeds that first articulated the biblical concept of being united in "one, holy, catholic, apostolic church."[2]

We all understand, at least in some measure, how a physical body works. We understand that all the parts are interconnected. Paul, using this imagery, calls for unity among believers. Can one imagine a body made up of a single eye? he asks.

---

[2]Charles Colson and Ellen Santilli Vaughn, *The Body* (Dallas: Word, 1992), p. 68.

Of course not! Or a single ear? Ridiculous. So, we are all *inter*dependent; we are all *inter*connected. And we comprise that uniquely designed structure called the body of Christ. It is a mystical body, yes, but a body nonetheless.

Paul asks, "Don't you know that your bodies are members of Christ? Shall I take away then the members of Christ and make them members of a harlot?"

The word "harlot" sounds antiquated today, but throughout Scripture it is used to communicate unfaithfulness, wickedness, and blasphemy. God called Israel a harlot when the nation turned to idolatry. The idea connotes faithlessness, filth, disease, and the destruction of an intimate relationship. It conjures up images of the foulest act one can carry out against a committed relationship.

A promiscuous Christian violates the entire body of believers because we are all one. He or she drags all of us, albeit unwittingly, into the chamber of sin.

Can the foot enter a room and leave behind the torso and the shoulder? Can an arm and leg travel the continent and leave behind the other arm and leg? Can one part of the body engage in illicit sexual behavior and the rest of the body wait in the foyer? It can't be done. Sexual behavior requires the presence of the entire body. It invokes responses from the soul and the spirit.

So what does all of this mean in the context of sexual sin in a believer's life? It means that the entire body, the church, is involved when a member commits sexual sin. The effects of sexual sin within the body of Christ may not be immediately visible; they may remain dormant for years. When disease infiltrates the human body, symptoms may be vague at first, perhaps indistinguishable, but as time passes they become quite obvious. If no steps are taken to identify and treat the condition, the disease worsens until the body is without strength, without power.

So it is within a spiritual body ravaged by sexual sin. A general sense of confusion and disorientation is almost always the first symptom. But it is often vague and unsubstantiated so it is easy to ignore. And the sin continues, slowly weakening the body even more.

Using another metaphor, Colson further clarifies the concept. The body, he says, is gathered into "confessing communities to fulfill His mission— that is, to administer the sacraments, preach the Word, and make disciples. Thus, immediately after Pentecost, Christ established the pattern: Individual believers were to gather into particular communities. . . . Its recruitment is universal, but it has to be broken down into visible fighting units."[3]

And it is within these "fighting units," the local churches, that we see the virulent effects of sexual sin. It is in these microcosms that the agony of moral failure is most deeply felt and most intimately observed. Imagine a "fighting unit" camped within sight of the enemy. Imagine a member of that unit sneaking out to commune with the enemy, spending his energy and strength enjoying the physical comforts offered to him in the enemy's camp. Imagine the sense of violation that the rest of the unit would feel upon learning that their comrade had been carousing with those whose goal was to destroy them!

---

[3]Ibid., p. 68.

In military terms, such behavior is called "fraternizing with the enemy." It carries serious consequences because it undermines the morale of the entire unit and suggests the very real possibility of betrayal. Even if only one member spent time with the enemy, the entire group is threatened. One person's act injures the entire company.

Taking Colson's imagery a step further, imagine that it was the company commander who slipped away from his soldiers and went to sleep with the enemy. Imagine the unit's anger and fear upon discovery of their leader's actions. Sexual intercourse is a kind of intimacy unmatched by any other physical act. And through sexual promiscuity a person chooses intimacy with the enemy rather than the one he or she claims to love.

David, after his sin with Bathsheba, sobbed before God with shame. His heartbreak throbs in his cry, "Against you, you only, have I sinned" (Psalm 51:4). Against God only, David says. Not against Bathsheba or Uriah or the nation of Israel whom he led. But against God only.

We have often heard pastors and teachers quote that prayer, suggesting that it should be our pattern for the prayer of confession. But are they right? In this period of history we call the Church Age, when believers are called the body of Christ, is David's prayer appropriate?

David, for all his devotion to God, had no comprehension of the mystery of the church. It would not be made clear until long after David's departure from this life. And so, David, while he was "a man after God's own heart," had no sense of being a part of a larger whole. He had no inkling that one day there would be a unit of believers that Christ would call His body.

And what of his prayer a bit later: "Do not . . . take your Holy Spirit from me" (Psalm 51:11)? Should we who enjoy the permanent indwelling presence of the Holy Spirit pray this prayer also simply because David prayed it?

David, in confessing sexual sin, confessed it to God and acknowledged that his sin was against God. But today, because each believer is a part of the mystical body of Christ, a confession of sexual sin is lacking if it does not acknowledge the injury inflicted upon that body.

Perhaps the prayer of confession for sexual sin should be modeled after Paul's New Testament teaching rather than David's Old Testament prayer. Perhaps the prayer of the adulterer ought to include something like this: "I have sinned against my Creator and Redeemer, and I have also sinned against the body He created, the church, which He has charged with the solemn task of testifying to His glory. I recognize that in opening my physical body to sexual sin, I have exposed the larger spiritual body, the church, to the effects of betrayal. I recognize my sin against *the body* as well as my sin against my heavenly Father."

Such an acknowledgment does not take anything away from the prayer of confession. Rather, it brings more weight to bear upon the act of repentance, for it recognizes the wider range of our sin, the utter horror of it for the children of God. It sends us not only to the heavens to seek forgiveness at the throne of grace; it also sends us to the body to seek reconciliation and the rebuilding of the trust and intimacy that has been damaged by infidelity.

In *Christianity Today*, David Neff wrote that "dalliance, like no other sin, destroys trust. . . . When the dike is breached by adultery, spouse and children can drown in the tide of pain. And the ripples and eddies of hurt reach far beyond the immediate family."[4]

Interdependence is the byword of the physical body. It is also the byword of the spiritual body. Our actions as individuals affect the entire congregation, those gathered in the local church as well as those who are part of the universal church. And no actions affect us all more drastically than sexual promiscuity.

Ted and Ryan led their church through the process of healing and restoration, but months later they were still grappling with questions and lingering feelings of personal failure. They felt they should have known; that they should have been able to prevent it. They wondered if maybe they had preached grace too often and judgment not often enough.

Their staff continues to ask questions. They wonder if they are doing all they can to ensure that this kind of tragedy will never occur again within their fighting unit.

The eddies of hurt swirl around people like Ted and Ryan. These are not baby Christians who were struggling to establish their faith when a trusted leader failed them. These are elders, mature believers who have walked the narrow path for many years. But still, after more than a year, they struggle to find relief from the pain inflicted when their pastor/colleague/friend fell into sexual sin.

---

[4]David Neff, "Are All Sins Equal?" *Christianity Today* (November 20, 1987).

A fighting unit is weakened. The bride of Christ is sullied. And the individual believer who sinned has dragged the entire body, unwittingly, into union with a harlot. This is the great horror of sexual sin. Its damage is neither easily forgotten nor quickly repaired. Its consequences stretch into eternity.

Part I

Voices

1

Voices From the Bottom of the Heap

Is It Ever Really Over?

Beverly sank wearily into a pew at the back of the church and stretched out in her dust-covered jeans. For a few quiet moments she stared across the empty auditorium and focused on the pulpit from which her husband preached.

Well, Lord, here we are celebrating Jim's twenty years in the ministry. You truly are a God of new beginnings. If I haven't said it yet today, thanks for moving us here after all that horrible trouble and for giving Jim another chance to pastor. We know we've been blessed, Lord. We don't take it lightly.

Rarely did Beverly enjoy a quiet moment without thoughts of the past demanding her attention. As she stared forward, a woman with a shock of gray hair popped in a side door near the platform.

"Beverly dear, are you in here? Hadn't we better see to those pictures?"

Oh, mercy yes. The pictures. Beverly had been on her way to Jim's office to search for loose photos to use in a slide presentation. Reluctantly she left her pew. "Coming, Millie. I've got the keys."

Minutes later Beverly was rummaging through

Jim's desk drawers past old bulletins, sermon notes, basketball schedules, and car wash receipts. Finding nothing in the first drawer, she opened the next.

And there she found them. Not hidden, not covered. Horrible, sickening, condemning pictures mocked her from the open drawer. Pictures of Jim and the woman from his previous church. Of Jim and his current church secretary.

In that tragic instant, Beverly's life as she knew it changed forever. Stunned by the cold reality of truth, she knew there would be no more chances.

Jim had again fallen into sexual sin. While preaching one way of life, he had chosen another for himself—one that risked the loss of his family, his ministry, his personal integrity, his inner peace.

An Isolated Case?

Sadly, this is not an isolated case. Christ's body, the church, is being violated again and again by adultery and fornication. In *The Sexual Christian* author Tim Stafford cites a study that says "religious people are as non-monogamous as anyone else" and that twenty-three percent admit to having had extramarital intercourse.[1] We, the body of Christ, are called to holy living and are empowered by God the Holy Spirit. Yet we are allowing sin, sexual sin, to contaminate us.

This is a book about consequences and healing. It's about the effects of sin on people like Beverly and Jim, their family, and their church. It's about people in the congregation—people who love the leaders who have failed them. And it is about hope

---

[1] Tim Stafford, *The Sexual Christian* (Wheaton, Ill.: Victor, 1989), p. 192.

and assurance. Assurance that God is indeed transcendent and that His eternal purposes cannot be thwarted, even by those whose lives betray their faith.

Hardly a week passes that we don't learn of some pastor/spiritual leader who has admitted to committing sexual sin. It may be adultery, often with a married woman in his congregation. It may be inappropriate sexual behavior with a young woman in the youth group. It may be living a separate life of sexual promiscuity outside the church.

Whatever the offense, the news spreads. And the church, local and universal, is . . . is what? Shocked? Perhaps that was the right word a few years ago. We used to be shocked by such revelations. But as reports mount, we are no longer shocked that such gross sin occurs among respected and renowned Christian leaders.

Again we cite the statistics from Tim Stafford's book. Twenty-three percent of the religious people surveyed admitted to having extramarital intercourse, as did twelve percent of the pastors while in ministry. These numbers are greatly disturbing, but it is equally disturbing that when such a fall occurs attention tends to focus on the already highly visible and powerful leader, to the exclusion of a hurting spouse and a very confused congregation. A congregation which generally responds in one of two ways: a knee-jerk dismissal and a frenzied "get him out of here!" or a misguided attempt to downplay the sin and continue the ministry uninterrupted.

What About the Ripple Effect?

While in some cases the injuries of those most directly wounded do receive a measure of attention, the injuries of many more have gone unrecognized and unattended. Wounded but ignored, the rest of the church—the members, the faithful worshipers, the children, the laity, and the staff—all stand quietly by, weakened, tentative, and unsure. And they ask:

- Will I ever again be able to trust a spiritual leader?
- Will I ever be willing to accept authority in spiritual matters when offered by a pastor or youth leader?
- Will I again be willing to receive the bread and the wine from the hand of one who stands before me?
- Will there come a day when I can participate in singing without harboring reservations toward the one leading me? Without questioning his sincerity and wondering about his life outside the church?

These are the questions that plague the wounded and that interfere with genuine, unreserved worship.

And these are the questions you have asked if you've felt the sudden panic and nausea born of a pastor's infidelity. If you've been confronted by boldface headlines, special news reports, or frantic phone calls, each more unbelievable than the last, and if you've desperately wanted to face that person one more time and look into his eyes, searching for the pastor you thought you knew, anxious for some affirmation that would wipe all the ugliness away.

We are, collectively, a hurting congregation. We are children and babes in Christ too fragile to survive a leader's moral fall unless strong arms are there to catch us. We are adolescents struggling with our sexuality who see the one who prodded us to be sexually pure admit to sexual impurity as though it were too hard even for him to resist. We are emotionally vulnerable adults who have depended on our pastor for support and counseling, teaching and guidance, and who suddenly find ourselves isolated and untrusting.

We are deacons and elders left to make important decisions both for our church and for our fallen pastor and his family, needing strength to carry out this difficult job of healing and restoration while we ourselves need it and while the world outside scrutinizes and questions every decision.

We are Christian leaders, both ordained and lay, who need to hear the victims speak. Who may need a reminder of our own responsibility to the church and to the Lord, a reminder of how every fall pulls others down into a heap, burying some so deeply they may never get up.

The Story Behind the Story

In the upcoming chapters you will hear the rest of Beverly's story, how she survived her husband's infidelity and learned to rejoice in the faithfulness of God.

You will meet two pastors whose hearts broke over their associates' sexual promiscuity. You will hear them express pain, confusion, and self-doubt, and you will share in their victory as they pronounce, loudly and with praise, that God is still God, no matter what.

You will meet congregants, teachers, and co-workers, all of whom have experienced the pain of deep disappointment as they learned that their respected, well-loved pastors were engaged in promiscuity.

You will see the path others have blazed toward their own spiritual restoration, and perhaps you too will want to set out for that place. Perhaps you too will be able to once again believe that the good work begun in you through Christ will continue, unabated, regardless of the failure of human leaders.

You will be given freedom to mourn, for sin breaks hearts and causes intense sadness. You will meet a congregation that mourned together in a Sunday morning worship service, acknowledging in front of the entire church that sin had been committed and that the whole body needed to be healed.

We have written this book to minister to the church, to wage war against the sin of adultery, and to issue a call to moral purity.

When Jim chose to fall (and yes, it was his choice; sin is always a choice), everyone around him fell as well—his wife, their children, the relatives, the church leaders, the congregation, his past congregation, friends and acquaintances, the community. Their falls were different from his; they did not fall into sin. Some fell into disillusionment and some into distrust and anger. Others fell into rationalization of their own immoral behavior—gossip, hate, or even a loss of faith. One after another they all fell down the hill and into the heap.

Voices of the Wounded

And coming from the bottom of the pile can be heard the dazed and shaky voices of the innocent, the bystanders, the victims, quietly asking:

How did I get here?
How badly am I hurt?
Who else is in this pile?
Can I stand up?
I don't feel like getting up. Can I just stay put?
How in the world did I end up in this heap? I've been
    minding my own business. How did this happen?
Was I blind? Was I stupid? Why didn't I see the
    signs?

Don't be too hard on yourself. You weren't blind. Maybe you simply weren't looking for trouble. You weren't looking for sin; you weren't prepared when it hit. Christians are taught to have hope. To expect the best. To think on whatever is good and lovely and pure. And when an incident here or there troubles us, we wait on God to take care of things.

But in this case I must have been a little too trusting. A little too naive.

Is it possible for Christians to ever be too trusting? Should we not continually focus on the best in people while consciously refusing to entertain judgmental thoughts and suspicions? To err on the side of too much trust rather than too little sounds like a good definition of Christian love.

I can't stop wondering if this was partly my fault.

Are you the one who committed the adultery? Did you set up their rendezvous? Did you lie to his wife? Did you run around removing all the warning signs?

Be careful not to add false guilt to the pile of rubble you're in. Yes, this is certainly a time for honest emotion and wise appraisal, but healing cannot progress if we keep adding garbage to the mess we're in.

How badly am I hurt?

Right now you are in great pain. Your heart has been broken. The news of your pastor's fall has sent you into shock. Don't jump up too quickly and assume you're okay. Stay still, gather your thoughts and feelings, and assess your injuries.

Who else is on this pile?

Falling the farthest and buried the deepest lies the errant pastor. Next to him lies his wife, and beside them are their children and relatives. Then close friends, the church board, the staff, church members, the congregation at large, neighbors and acquaintances, and so on. In all probability, everyone you know is somewhere on the heap, and those at the bottom are pressed by the heaviest weight.

Can I stand up?

Psalm 40 tells us that the Lord sees us and hears us and lifts us up out of the depth of our circumstances and makes us stand firm.

You will gain strength from the promises of God and from those around you. No, it won't be easy. You are stiff, shaken, and bruised. But eventually you will stand. And then you will walk. And one day you will even run and leap and dance.

You are a child of Almighty God and you were not created to lie buried in the consequences of sin. You are dressed in the armor of God, which makes you "able to stand" (Ephesians 6).

Standing up sounds awfully hard. Maybe I'll just stay put. Who will miss me?

It's your choice. God provides the strength, but you must make the decision. Whether you choose to remain face down in the rubble or to rise up and run, your life will be a testimony. It is up to you to choose which type of testimony it will be.

Who will miss you? The answer to that is easy. We all will, the whole body of Christ, and particularly those around you. Some may be more seriously injured than you. Some might not have been wearing their full armor. And some might never have met the Savior, who alone is able to make them stand. As unfair as this sounds, it's true: If you don't get up, you'll be allowing the effects of the sin to continue.

You are much too precious to the Lord and to the body to remain useless after this fall.

You Are Not Alone

Lest you think your situation is rare, be assured that it is not. The church is producing a mound of casualties to rival the Andes. Everywhere we went in researching this book we encountered victims still suffering the effects of a leader's fall.

We went to a professor to gain scriptural insight, and we learned about a pastor whom he had walked through spiritual recovery after an affair.

We asked a psychologist about those who blame the spouse when adultery occurs, and we learned of her personal struggle to attend church due to her knowledge of her pastor's infidelity.

We talked to a pastor known for his emphasis on open and honest communication in ministry, and we saw the grief he continues to suffer over a former staff member's promiscuity.

We interviewed another pastor concerning social programs within the church, and we ended up talking about his pastor/friend's recent confession of adultery.

Everyone we talked to told a story. Everyone knew heartache.

A small voice within us whispers, "What? Don't you know that your bodies are members of Christ? That your body is the temple of the Holy Spirit? That you have been bought with a price?"

Do we still not know this, or have we been listening to a lie? Have we forgotten sin's power to kill and separate and weaken and destroy?

We have written this book as a guide to help you confront the enormity of sexual sin in the church and as a platform from which the victims—the spouses, families, and congregations often left alone in their hurt and confusion—can voice their feelings, thoughts, and prayers. While we love our fallen leaders and desire nothing less than their full, sincere healing and restoration to the body, our desire and purpose here is to minister to those who have been wounded in the wake of their leader's fall.

In these opening chapters, some we spoke to will tell how it feels to lie at the bottom of the heap. For Beverly, her wound was opened again when she discovered the graphic pictures in a drawer in her husband's study.

2

A Forever Tragedy

Aftershocks

"I boarded the train and settled into my seat, both nervous and excited to begin the trip ahead. With a few quick jerks the train pushed slowly into the night, and I calmly embarked on my journey, confident of my destination and the safety of the train. Suddenly, BOOM! There was an explosion. I was propelled through a window and dumped on the ground. I lay perfectly still, waiting, afraid to look up, listening for signs of life in the darkness. Finally a conductor came along, put out his hand, and said, 'Don't worry. It's safe now. We've fixed everything. Time to get back on board.' I hesitated, but for some reason I allowed him to lead me back to my seat. Again the train jerked to a start and rolled into the night. I eased back into the cushions, now lumpy from being patched, and stared anxiously out a window held together by tape. I tried to relax but refused to close my eyes. Then, BOOM! Another explosion."

For Beverly Carter, this dream symbolized her marriage, a marriage fraught with explosions. Through twenty-one years, two children, and three churches, Beverly Carter's calling had been that of a pastor's wife. Yet those same twenty-one years had dragged her through a husband's infidelity and faked suicide, through the loss of close friends and rewarding ministry, and eventually through a divorce.

Looking back at such ambushed dreams and expectations would make even the most confident Christian wonder where she had gone wrong, where she had misread God or subjugated His leading to her own personal will, or to youthful passions and romanticized scripts.

Beverly's story disallows any pat answers.

No Warning Signs

While in seminary, Jim officially proposed, and Beverly earnestly sought assurance that this marriage was God's plan for her. She claimed Catherine Marshall's prayer of relinquishment as her own, eager to empty herself of any feelings and emotions that could hinder God's leading.

Beverly's moment of inner assurance still exists in vivid memory. It arrived, the proverbial bolt from the blue, not during prayer or some meaningful discussion, but while out on a casual walk with Jim, the two of them laughing, holding hands. Suddenly, in one off-beat moment, Beverly felt her burden of uncertainty lifted. Peace came as a gift as God let her know that it was indeed His will for this marriage to take place.

In hindsight such a memory gives birth to many questions. If their marriage had God's blessing, what went wrong? Had she misread God? Had she mistaken tingling hormones for His quiet, small voice? Often during their marriage, when day-to-day difficulties would arise, Beverly's response would be: "God, You told me to marry him and I know You've got things under control." At those times she never doubted God's will. The doubting didn't come until twenty years later, when Jim confessed to adultery.

This created a great dilemma for her: If God truly had led her to marry Jim, knowing full well what eventual heartache awaited, then had He not on some level set her up for all this pain? During infrequent moments of despair and aloneness, Beverly wrestled to understand what it meant to have absolute faith in an Almighty God who knowingly led her into a marriage doomed to fail.

Sorting It All Out

But for Beverly, detonating the issue took a reversal of view. Instead of asking "Why me, Lord?" she learned to ask "Why *not* me?" In a sin-cursed system where God's will for our lives works itself out through decaying bodies in a decaying world, where our lives are continually challenged by the disobedience and rebellion of others as well as our own, Beverly came to realize that she was not the one person on earth immune to the effects of sin. That she could not expect to be exempt from bad things happening and from disappointments and failures. That there's no promise anywhere that says any of us will escape being hurt by the sins of another.

Sin had much to destroy in the ministry of Jim and Beverly Carter. Married during seminary, Jim began his ministry as the music director of a mid-sized Bible church in Florida. Shortly before graduation he was called to pastor a tiny church in the Midwest. There this young couple built a successful ministry that spanned the next seventeen years, where, as Beverly tells it, Jim was well loved and well thought of, a warm and empathetic leader continually affirmed by his growing congregation, an excellent Bible teacher and a gifted pastor.

Warm and caring Jim—a good husband, loving father, committed pastor. He serving the Lord, she serving right alongside him. Most "before" pictures emphasize the negative—straggly hair, no makeup, thin smile—all guaranteed to reveal an incredible transformation in the "after" photo. But their "before" photo looked well-groomed and contented.

"I look back and wonder how I could have been so blind. If you had written on the wall in capital letters, JIM IS HAVING AN AFFAIR, I wouldn't have believed it," said Beverly.

Even when truth did appear as clearly as writing on the wall, Beverly refused to acknowledge it.

Discovering the Truth

One afternoon following a long morning of refereeing preschoolers at the church day-care center, Beverly came home early to find the back door locked—a door that normally remained unlocked during the day. Although she was almost certain Jim was home, it being his one day off during the week, Beverly chose not to knock and possibly wake him. She spent a few moments rifling through her purse for some keys and then opened the door. There in her kitchen stood a woman from the congregation staring off down the hall as Jim came shuffling in wearing his bathrobe.

Beverly mumbled a few words of greeting before heading downstairs to start the laundry. She heard muffled voices and a door closing, followed by gentle, soft footsteps descending the stairs. Jim opted for small talk. When Beverly responded in silence, his monologue of reasoning began.

. . . The woman had only stopped by to discuss some church business. He had gotten up late and not bothered to dress. After all, this was his only day off. He shouldn't have to get dressed, but he couldn't turn people away . . .

In retrospect there's no misreading the scene. This woman had come to visit Beverly's husband on his morning off, knowing he was there all alone. And how did she know Jim was alone? Because Beverly was caring for her child at the preschool. She was his teacher.

Yet Beverly didn't suspect anything. After Jim's explanation, she offered a simple scolding, warning him that the next time a woman came to visit he'd better take the time to get dressed and that he'd better be more conscious of how these situations could look to others.

Beverly refused to be suspicious of wrongdoing. The husband she loved she also knew as a pastor, as one whose character and honesty were supported and established by his teaching and by his position as a spiritual leader. As for the woman, Beverly considered her one of the more spiritual of the congregation. She was quick to share a testimony or teach a class and possessed a proven heart for evangelism. Beverly's concept of these two individuals made it impossible for her to read the sit-

uation as anything other than a serious but innocent lapse in judgment.

So she fled to the basement to do laundry. To
seek comfort in routine, as though by performing
the mundane she could steer life back on track.
Nothing changed, nothing threatened. And yet,
neither the comfort of routine nor the facade of innocence could silence the niggling doubt that in-
truded upon her consciousness.

He doeth all things Well

Dealing With the Truth

Soon after this incident the church sent Jim on
a trip around the world that separated him from
Beverly for several weeks. For Beverly, this was the
beginning of inner discovery and honesty. Women
would come up to her on Sundays and say, "Don't
you miss Pastor something awful?" And she would
say to herself, "Well, no. Not too much." She began
to realize that life went along pretty much the same
whether Jim was home or not, and that somehow
their busy routine had replaced marital intimacy
and passion.

Shortly after Jim's return, all of life changed for
Beverly. The youth pastor found Jim kissing a
woman in the church basement. The woman
claimed to be welcoming him home, and when the
elders confronted them she took all the blame.

Facing the Facts

During this time Beverly was scheduled to enter
the hospital for tests. Acute, advancing arthritis
had long plagued Beverly and it could no longer be
controlled with medication and heating pads.

About an hour before they were to leave for the hospital, Jim took Beverly to the basement to talk. Then he started to cry.

"Beverly, there are some rumors circulating and I'd like you to hear about them from me rather than from one of your friends." There was a short pause and total silence as Beverly's attention moved from her physical pain to sick inner fear. Jim told her about the kiss and named the woman he had been caught with—the same woman Beverly had discovered in her kitchen months earlier.

He claimed that this was a one-time-only kiss, that there was nothing else between them, but Beverly couldn't stop asking questions. She pressed hard for the truth, and finally he admitted that yes, there had been one affair, ten years earlier, with another woman in the church.

Instant, intense pain consumed Beverly. She felt as if he had physically thrown her on the floor and kicked her in the stomach. Finally forced to face the truth, Beverly wanted the details. If she had to deal with it, she wanted to deal with all of it, the total truth, and not have to live in fear of daily revelations.

After much prodding and cross-examination, she eventually learned of at least three previous affairs, and Jim finally began naming names.

The thought of trying to collect the fragments of her life and heal her marriage overwhelmed Beverly, but leaving Jim wasn't an option. He appeared genuinely repentant, and Beverly dearly wanted to relegate all this ugly horror to the past. With everything out in the open, with counseling and prayer, surely their marriage could be salvaged. Her family, her ministry, her life as she knew it depended on such healing. She had little choice but to believe in Jim's sincerity.

Living With the Horrible Secret

The next eight months were a living hell. Jim had slept with three women who were still active in the congregation, and now Beverly had to pretend as if nothing had happened. She had to continue teaching and singing and organizing potlucks as if everything was fine, while wondering all the time how many others knew the situation.

On the one hand Beverly desperately needed the prayers and support of her friends, but she just as desperately needed them not to know about anything. She wanted to talk, and she didn't want to talk. And some days she *couldn't* talk.

Jim and Beverly's situation was being handled by two staff members, an elder, and their wives, all of whom had pledged secrecy. Jim agreed to leave the church as quickly as possible, but leaving the ministry was never made a stipulation.

Eight months passed before Jim and Beverly were called to a new church hundreds of miles across the country. Eight months was too long to keep things quiet. By the time they left, the rumor mill had exploded, making Beverly as much a target for anger and blame as Jim was, since she then was seen as part of the cover-up.

Friends she had loved and counted on now turned away due to their own hurt and pain over Jim's betrayal and unfaithfulness. For Beverly, that was the worst hurt. She had expected the pain of Jim's betrayal, but she hadn't expected to be hurt by the people she needed most. Once a trusted friend, she was now an object of criticism and pity. She wondered continually what they were saying and whom they were blaming. Did they think she hadn't been a good enough wife?

Taking the Blame on Herself

One painful encounter occurred with the husband of one of the women with whom Jim had been involved. This husband let Beverly know, to her face, that he assumed the affair had happened because Beverly was cold. Beverly stood there quietly and let him talk, while all the time she wanted to scream, "What about you? How hot could it have been at your house?"

Yet even Beverly joined in that chorus of blame and asked the same questions of her marriage. Jim had never complained to her about their sex life. Had the lack of passion existed because he had not been satisfied, or because he had found passion elsewhere?

While Beverly was in the hospital one of Jim's former lovers called Beverly to reassure her that her own marriage "was better than ever," and that she was no longer interested in Jim.

"Great," thought Beverly, "and my marriage is down the tubes." But she forced herself to visit the woman following her release from the hospital, intending to forgive her and reestablish as comfortable a relationship as possible. It seemed terribly important to get that initial meeting over with.

Since they had last visited, the woman had moved, and their time together ended up being a tour of her beautiful new home, accompanied by a running commentary on how well her marriage was going. Beverly nodded and smiled her way through, all the while thinking, "Lord, why does she have the new house and the good marriage when she's the one who committed adultery?"

For this woman, the affair had long been over. She had come to terms with it. Her life had started to heal while Beverly's hurt was still fresh. They ended that day by claiming to be friends, but there was no real friendship after that. All subsequent encounters brought renewed, stabbing pain.

Leaving the Only Support She Knew

And so Jim and Beverly drove off to begin a new pastorate, leaving behind a church Beverly loved, friends she had known for seventeen years, and a home and ministry that had framed both her marriage and her self-worth. She had gone through weddings and baby showers and illnesses with people who now seemed so distant. She had comforted them, prayed with them, shared holidays with them, and cared for their children. And now it was over . . . because Jim had to leave.

Today Beverly counsels women caught in this situation to expect once-close friends to turn away. Maybe they can't accept what happened, maybe they can't handle it, maybe its existence threatens their own fragile marriages. Many friends will turn their backs. But even as they do, she encourages, others will draw near. For Beverly there was one acquaintance, one staff member, who became her lifeline; who provided both her and Jim with wonderful support. At a time when others seemed to be saying, "We're outraged that you're such a horrible sinner," this person genuinely loved and prayed for them both. And that meant everything.

Yet how difficult it was for Beverly to get back on that "train" and begin once more her journey into the night. Ahead lay a new church, an unfamiliar city, and a congregation of strangers. And there in that car, surrounded by her confused and broken family, she traveled alone.

Beverly knew that the move, while it was an escape and an opportunity for a fresh start, in no way guaranteed victory over the sin. The past tragically separated her from the one person she most needed to be close to, the one person who should have been able to provide her emotional support. There sat Beverly and Jim, husband and wife, two no longer one, two now tragically separated by sin.

And in that same car sat her children—children needing her protection, craving security, and for whom she felt forced to keep up a facade of excitement and anticipation and a show of support for their father.

Such a show was not easy.

Their house had been sold and the moving van scheduled when Jim's new church got wind of his troubles. Rather than opt for the easy solution and tell Jim to stay put, the church allowed the family to complete their move, planning to deal with the problem once Jim arrived. Unfortunately, that church already had serious problems and it soon split, leaving Jim with half a congregation desperate for a pastor. He and Beverly then settled into the ministry once again—a new church, a new life, and a forgiven past.

Reopening the Wound

Then came plans for an anniversary party to celebrate Jim's twenty years in the ministry. This was when Beverly initiated the picture hunt to compile a commemorative album and slide presentation for the event. Her search led her to that unlocked desk drawer in Jim's office.

And to the pictures. Love letters and pictures. Pictures of Jim and the woman from his first church. Notes from his current secretary. Graphic, incriminating pictures sitting right next to last Sunday's sermon mocked her from that unlocked drawer. No simple welcome-home kisses here. No room for misunderstanding. No simple excuses.

"The first time Jim cheated on me I was heart-broken," Beverly said. "But this time I was furious. This time *I* was the one seeing the evidence. No elders, no gossips, just me—face-to-face with proof made blatantly accessible. How could he have done this to me? How could he have ruined our last chance to make our lives work?"

At the same time that Beverly was discovering the pictures, Jim was attending a conference in Arizona. He came home spouting new commitments and resolutions for the future, but by then they meant nothing. Beverly had become much harder to lie to. Her feelings were numb, her trust depleted. No matter how deeply she wanted to believe his promises, her days of desperate optimism were gone.

So what does a pastor's wife do when her marriage seems over? In conservative circles, when a pastor divorces, he simply can't move out, divide up property, and visit the kids. His job is over and his future bleak. For ministers, "D" is the scarlet letter that marks them for life. While many congregations may accept and forgive him, they'll never again be willing to consider his resume. And if, as is true in some cases, the church holds the mortgage to their house and the title to their van, there might be precious little left with which to begin a new life. When faced with such huge ramifications, how long can the spouse persevere? How deep must she bury her own pain and resentment for the sake of her family and their future?

An Effort to Redeem the Marriage

Until now, Jim had resisted counseling. When you have been the counselor, being the counselee isn't easy. To whom does a pastor go for help? To a secular psychologist who has no understanding of sin and grace and of the healing of the Spirit? Or to another Christian counselor, someone considered a peer? To whom will he ever disclose such extreme moral failings? To whom will he reveal the demons he struggles against?

Unfortunately, many go nowhere, except as a last resort. And sin and secrecy begin taking their toll. The pastor stands preaching on a darkened stage, lit by a tightly focused spotlight. The congregation sees only the man as the leader. Then the tiny pinpoint of light widens to reveal the first hint of indiscretion. Snap. Someone flicks a switch and the floodlights go on. The darkness is obliterated; the life is exposed. And we look in horror at the man surrounded by his sin.

Jim had heard the switch. The spotlight was widening, and he was powerless to stop it. He consented to counseling, and he and Beverly both started attending sessions, at times as a couple, at times individually.

More Secrets, More Pain

Again Beverly found herself blown from the train. She learned of a secret trip Jim had made back East to be with his former lover, and she saw copies of love letters he had written. That's when Beverly gave up emotionally. She had no intention of getting back on that train.

While in her mind the marriage was over, Beverly did nothing physically to separate from Jim. Her counselor had stressed the importance of not making major decisions until the dust settled, claiming that no decision made while reeling backwards is a good one. Beverly agreed to trust his wisdom, and she returned home with Jim to figure out what to do next. Right then, the only thing they were sure of was that Jim must resign from the church and seek secular work. Then, with the help of their counselor, Jim and Beverly laid out a plan for the following week. On Monday, there in the counselor's office, he would tell the children what was happening and why. On Thursday he would tell the elders and resign. On Friday morning the family would leave for Colorado for a counseling center for ministers and their families.

"During counseling Jim told me that he could finally admit to himself that he no longer loved me, but he still did not want a divorce," Beverly said. "I asked him, 'Do you mean to say that when you *thought* you loved me you couldn't be faithful, but now that you know you *don't* love me I'm supposed to believe you *will* be faithful?' He nodded his head yes, and I shook mine in disbelief."

They returned home with little resolved. Jim's resignation hadn't yet been made public, and on

Wednesday of that week he said he had an appointment with a couple in a neighboring county to discuss their wedding. Beverly asked why he wasn't meeting them at his office, and Jim said they were being married in a home and he needed to see it.

As he stood at the front door ready to leave, Beverly noticed him looking at her strangely. She had no way of knowing that this was the last moment of their life together.

Escape From Reality

When Beverly went to bed that night Jim had not returned, but that wasn't unusual. About midnight the phone rang. Jim's secretary's husband wanted to speak to Jim. Beverly got up and searched the house, but Jim wasn't there. When she went back to the phone, the frantic husband said he suspected Jim and his wife of running away together.

At 7:30 the next morning, following a sleepless night, Beverly received a call from the police. Jim's car had been found in a nearby lake, but divers had found no body. This didn't surprise the police. They told Beverly that all indications pointed to a staged suicide. Most likely Jim had run away.

When local papers reported the abandoned car and the dragging of the lake, two private detectives came forward with stories of recent meetings with Jim in which he had asked advice on staging a disappearance and assuming a new identity. The second detective brought with him a tape recording, a message from Jim, explaining how and why he was planning to commit suicide and make it look like an accident.

In a distraught voice, Jim described himself as "ruined and humiliated . . . having lost my job, my career, and my house." He said he could not bear to face "everybody that I have hurt so much." He admitted his plan to drown himself and make it appear accidental and explained that he had "retained a person to make this tape available" in the event that someone was falsely accused of causing the accident, or in case he wasn't found. "I don't want people to think I'm missing or I've disappeared," he said.

He wanted people to think he was dead.

At first Beverly could almost believe the suicide report. Jim had been terribly despondent. He had lost everything. And while the Jim she had married years earlier would never have done something like this, she now realized that the old Jim no longer existed. He'd become a stranger to her.

In Jim's warped thinking, he truly believed everyone would be better off if they thought him dead. He did change his identity and begin a new life in another state. He went alone, however. His secretary didn't join him until almost two years later, after her divorce was final.

Help From Everywhere

In the early weeks after Jim's disappearance, Beverly led the children in an effort to reestablish some sort of family routine. She made herself get up every day, putting one foot in front of the other, working around the gaping hole in the fabric of their lives. Four months later, Jim called his parents and his children to let them know he was alive.

He refused to speak to Beverly.

How has Beverly survived the trauma? How has she managed to hold together her home and family, starting back to work full time in a beginning secretarial position when one child was a sophomore in college and the other was in high school?

Jim abandoned Beverly. God didn't.

There are many stories Beverly could tell about God's provision. Money came from total strangers, from at least three other churches, and from missionaries. God seemed to choose remote sources to remind Beverly that the gifts really did come from Him and not simply from friends. It was truly a faith-strengthening time, and it continues to be. God hasn't stopped giving. With that very first gift, from people she hadn't seen or heard from in twenty years, Beverly felt God wrapping His arms around her. His calm and gentle message was, "Don't worry, Bev, I'll take care of you. You don't have to know where it's coming from. I'll provide."

"You see," she explains, "when you've had a husband who has been unfaithful, you just thank God over and over that He is faithful. That He is *absolutely faithful.*"

To hurting wives and broken families whose pain is as devastating and whose self-esteem is as bruised as hers once was, Beverly has some things to say.

Counseling Is a Must

First, counseling is a must for both spouses. No matter what the husband says—that he's sorry, that it only happened once, that he has some group he's accountable to— the wife must *insist* that he go for counseling. This is especially important for pastors.

They need to be questioned by someone who's not intimidated or silenced by their position and authority.

It was during counseling that Beverly learned she should have stood up to Jim more often in their marriage and confronted him when his excuses and answers didn't satisfy her. Unfortunately, the ability to confront doesn't develop easily in young women raised on traditional principles of Christian womanhood. To Beverly, choosing *not* to confront was an act of spiritual strength and obedience, which somehow guaranteed that God would step in and make everything right, that God himself would confront Jim. But what happens when sin has made the still, small voice of God inaudible to a sinner? What happens when God has no audience? There are times when God works through our words as well as our silence.

Second, Beverly advises those in a position similar to hers to seek out someone who has survived, someone to stand as a symbol of hope. That is why Beverly is telling her story. By God's grace she has survived. Yes, she still struggles. She sometimes feels cheated—cheated out of growing old with her husband, of celebrating a twenty-fifth, a fortieth, and a fiftieth wedding anniversary, of sharing grandchildren. "There's a deep sadness for what I've missed," says Beverly, "and it's a tragedy. A forever tragedy."

But she has survived the tragedy.

Although Beverly has been angry with God, she's never doubted His love. God allowed Jim's fall, but He didn't cause it, she says. Sin caused it, and Beverly has learned to focus her anger on sin, to mourn that which ruins families and churches and ministries. To mourn the betrayal, the faithlessness, the sin that threatened to destroy her family and herself. But she's also seen the beauty of the flip side of betrayal. She's learned to be infinitely more thankful for God's faithfulness now that she knows so well the sorrow of being betrayed.

A Plea to Look at the Consequences

And what about spiritual leaders who are fighting Satan and temptation every day? What would Beverly tell those who are close to falling?

Her number one message would be, straight out, that *adultery destroys the family.* She would urge them to think of its effect on their children. When a father is a pastor, a child's whole spiritual identity is tied up in that relationship. He is the example, the conscience, the quiet voice at night by the bed, the spiritual authority in that child's world. When that relationship crumbles, it's not easily rebuilt.

When a pastor commits adultery, he loses trust and respect that may never be regained. Jim was so deceitful for so long that Beverly says she could never again respect him or give him her trust.

She once said to him, "You could have looked the world over and never found a more trusting wife than I." She *chose* to trust Jim, believing that if you trust and expect the best from someone, he will live up to your expectations. Yet now she doubts that, apart from God, she would ever be able to trust again.

Trust and Forgiveness

The difficult issue for Beverly was trust, not forgiveness. When Jim's story first broke, she grabbed every book she could find on forgiveness and came to accept it as a process. It comes in spurts. Beverly believes she truly was able to forgive Jim over time, but trust and respect are a different matter. She places them in separate categories. At this point they remain dead issues.

It is ironic that pastors are viewed by congregations as so morally strong that they would never succumb to adultery, when instead they are among the ones most often attacked by sexual temptation. Other women saw Jim only as the perfect husband, Beverly recalls, very warm and tender, always spiritually strong. He had a softness that melted them. He cried easily. And every time they saw him he was in a coat and tie, not cutting meat, not driving a truck, not fixing a toilet. While Beverly loved him in spite of his imperfections, to the other women he had none.

When Jim's imperfections were exposed and Beverly's life and marriage became the subject of public scrutiny, Beverly made a choice that to many seems surprising. When instinct told her to run, shake off the past, find a new community, and start again in a new church, after Jim's desertion, Beverly chose instead to remain within that same church, that same body of believers, and there begin her healing.

Godly elders led the congregation in nurturing Beverly. They became her support system. Her advice to other hurting spouses is to remain in the congregation where people already care for and love them if at all possible. Yes, there will be painful times to endure, but that pain is a given, regardless of whether they go or whether they stay. While instinct may urge them to hide in isolation, breaking all ties with those who already love them, doing so will only compound the losses.

The same can be said for relationships with in-laws. Beverly continues to be close to Jim's family, receiving wonderful love and support from them that has proven to be one of God's greatest blessings. Mercifully, though hearts were broken on both sides, these relationships have become a source of strength to all concerned.

Survival Is Possible

Today if you met Beverly you would soon come to know her as a godly woman, one who has wrestled with the Lord, who has been broken and survived, and who knows the grace of God. She's lovely, she's fun, and she's free from the day-to-day burden of a lying, wounding marriage.

Does Beverly believe she's happier than she might have been if her marriage had continued with Jim's infidelities kept secret?

Beverly's answer is immediate. "No. I can't say I'm happier, but I'm certainly more at peace. Yet I do believe it would have been better for the children if the marriage could have lasted. I only wish somehow they could have had their dad."

Yes, her children have had much to work through, but look at the mother God gave them. Look at the strength they will someday come to understand and the character they've witnessed in her.

Today Beverly's ministry continues with her children and within her church. Recently the church began a program based on Titus 2:4 that pairs older women with younger ones. The idea is to provide guidance and teaching through one-on-one relationships. They matched Beverly with a woman who is older than she—recently divorced, somewhat bitter, in need of a sensitive touch. For their first meeting they went to lunch, and when Beverly got out of the car, the woman said to her, "I certainly don't know why they put us together. It's like the blind leading the blind, isn't it?"

Hopefully that woman will come to know Beverly as you've gotten to know her through her story. Yes, Beverly was hurt. She trusted, and she was hurt again. She lost her husband and her life was turned upside-down.

But she stood and she survived.

And you could never call her blind.

3

A Parishioner's Story

"I grew up in a small town where everyone knew everyone else. Everybody was on the same party line. My grandma used to listen over the telephone and hear the gossip about the preachers. I grew up knowing what some preachers were doing and who they were doing it with."

Andrea wasn't naive. She believed preachers, "men of God," were just that: men. Not infallible potentates. She knew them to be capable of sexual sin, capable of adultery. Still, as an adult, she wasn't prepared to see her pastor slide into sexual promiscuity. She wasn't prepared to deal with the feelings of betrayal and outrage that assaulted her when she learned of his double life.

Andrea has not one story but two. Two separate accounts of pastors she knew well who ventured past the barriers of decency and into adultery. Pastors who violated their marriage vows and betrayed the trust of their congregations. In both cases, Andrea was close enough to observe the events and the principle players; close enough to get burned when the ministries exploded and the work went up in smoke.

"It's a parking lot now," Andrea said, referring

to the site of the church where she witnessed the first tragedy. Nothing remains but a concrete surface at a busy intersection in a major metropolitan city.

Before the bulldozers and the cement mixers came, an inter-denominational church stood on the site. It was led by respected Christian men educated at Baptist universities and conservative seminaries. Former Methodists, Presbyterians, Baptists, Assemblies, and Pentecostals comprised the congregation. Sharing a vision of world evangelism and a commitment to making a difference in their own community as well, the church built a television station, established a youth farm, founded a Bible college, and built a retirement care village. Supporting dozens of missionaries in foreign locations, they were a visible force for the Gospel in the U.S. and around the world.

"I'd been attending there for about two years when it happened," Andrea said, "and the church was like my family. I worked at the television station as a receptionist."

Andrea was part of the ministry team. She was paid no salary. Her work was considered a "faith ministry," which meant she had to raise her own support, as did all those who worked full-time for the church's outreach programs. But Andrea was willing. Watching God supply her needs in miraculous ways increased her faith and reaffirmed that she was doing what God wanted her to do.

When she learned that her pastor, a married man in his thirties, had been having an affair with a married woman in his congregation, Andrea was appalled. "The whole ministry disintegrated almost immediately," she said. "It splintered, unraveled in a matter of days after the news spread." Most of the people scattered, and what had been a large, loving congregation became a small, angry horde.

Protecting the Message

The pastor was quickly removed from leadership within the church, but ousting him from his position with the television ministry proved more difficult. Mortgage contracts and production agreements complicated the process. He stepped away from the pulpit without a fight, but he dug in his heels at the television production offices.

For Andrea, the pain of loss was excruciating. She had been an intercessor for that body, and as it quickly splintered and new allegiances formed that pitted member against member, friend against friend, she felt as though her own body were being broken into pieces.

People Andrea had been close to in the congregation expected her to be among those who would line up against the pastor. But Andrea didn't. She stayed at her job with the television station where the promiscuous pastor had stubbornly settled in. And she kept on working under his leadership.

"You have to understand," Andrea said, "I believed in the ministry, not the man. The message was what kept me together."

The message of the gospel. The message they were proclaiming on television. The message that taught redemption by faith. She was committed to its continued broadcast. She believed she was serving God, no one else. She was doing God's will.

"If the television ministry folded, one of two things would happen," she said. "First, the station could go black, meaning the message would be silenced. Or the station could go commercial."

Andrea didn't like either of those options. And so she determined to try to help keep the station on the air as long as possible. In spite of the minister's infidelity. In spite of her own heartbreak over the situation.

"I hated the hypocrisy of the pastor," Andrea said. "He had preached how to avoid the pitfalls while he was living in the pit."

And she hated the fear that troubled her.

"He'd been a spiritual giant to me," she said, "and it scared me. If he could fall, so could I."

Andrea voiced one of the great unspoken fears of congregations harmed by a leader's infidelity: If it can happen to a man of his stature, it can happen to me.

It may be difficult to understand Andrea's decision to stay with the television ministry, but her decision was not made lightly. Only after hours of struggle and prayer did she decide to stay. She chose to make herself vulnerable for the sake of the proclamation of the gospel. Vulnerable to misunderstanding and disappointment. This was God's will as Andrea understood it at that time.

Willing to be hurt again, Andrea stayed where she believed she could be of greatest use to the kingdom of God. Her priority: keep the message of salvation on the air waves.

Enough Is Enough

A few weeks after making her decision to stay with the television ministry, Andrea took a second painful blow. She was sitting at her desk when one of the secretaries down the hall called to her. "Andrea, come look at this—you won't believe it."

Andrea walked down the hall and turned the corner into the pastor's office. On the wall behind his desk was a life-sized photo of his lover. Blatantly flaunting his sin, he seemed to be daring anyone to condemn him.

While Andrea had no illusions about this man's repentance—she had sensed his stubbornness—she had hoped and prayed that his sin would begin to grieve him, as it grieved God. She had prayed that he would be restored to a faithful life, but now it was obvious to her that he had no desire for holiness. She was standing in the studio offices when he walked up to her, draped an arm across her shoulder, and leaned on her heavily.

"Don't do that," Andrea said, shrugging against him and pulling away. "We'll both fall over."

"We won't fall," he answered. "I know who you're leaning on."

The allusion wasn't lost on Andrea. She was the "good child," the one God would bless. The preacher was depending on that, on Andrea. In his thinking, she would be the vessel through which God would sustain this sadly weakened ministry.

Andrea's dilemma was terrible. She was an intercessor. She spent hours every day in prayer for this ministry, for its impact in the community, for each of the individuals involved in the production and presentation of the message. Since her leader couldn't approach the throne of God in his state of unconfessed sin, she felt a double need for her continued prayers and efforts on behalf of the ministry. She personally felt the burden of his sin.

Could she bear the weight of it? Would God have

her be the vessel through which He would guide and protect this work against the effects of its leader's sin? Should she stay, continuing to work for the station, carrying the needs of the ministry to the throne of grace? Should she abandon the work and the handful of others who, like Andrea, were trying to maintain a schedule of Christian programming? Were the faithful efforts of a few enough to counteract the faithlessness of one?

Earlier, Andrea had been certain that she should stay with the television work, but not anymore. She had reached a crossroads, that much she knew, but she didn't know which fork to take. In a gesture so like a loving Father, God took the decision out of her hands. A nationally known televangelist bought the station, and Andrea had no choice but to leave. Within days of the sale of the station, God provided Andrea a position with a legal firm and she moved her family to a suburb across town.

Was I an Enabler?

Years have passed since the church at the busy intersection was dissolved and the buildings razed to build a parking lot. But the pain Andrea still feels over her pastor's betrayal has not been as easy to get rid of as bricks and two-by-fours. Alongside the hurt are nagging questions that trigger self-doubt. "Did my staying enable the pastor to continue his sinful lifestyle?" she has asked many times. "Did I help or hinder the work of God by standing by him?"

Difficult questions. But Andrea is not the first to ask them. We can open the Bible to almost any book of history in the Old Testament and read about prophets who, while serving under wicked kings, faced the same awful dilemma. They agonized over the same questions. Wasn't it important to be a voice? If only one voice?

Out of the Frying Pan and Into the Fire

As soon as Andrea was settled in her new home, she joined a young nine-hundred-member church in her neighborhood. She was excited about its community ministries, its aggressive soul-winning philosophy, and the opportunities it offered her for involvement. Within a short time, she was team-teaching a large and growing Sunday school class for middle-aged women. She welcomed a handful of younger women, under thirty, who wanted to be a part of the group as well.

Roger Feldman, the pastor, was young and enthusiastic. His style and charisma had already begun attracting national attention. As an evangelist, he was among the most dynamic in his denomination, and his ministry was gaining momentum daily. In addition to the "old, old story," he had one of his own to tell about abuse, abandonment, and the power of God to lift the brokenhearted. But within two years, he was exposed as a fraud and a promiscuous sexual predator.

In hindsight, Andrea can see that signs of trouble abounded long before Roger was confronted with allegations of misconduct, but in the beginning she was enthralled by his powerful preaching and captivated by his personality. When she observed scenes that troubled her, she shrugged them off, unwilling to attach importance to them, unwilling even to imagine that Roger would behave in an inappropriate way.

More than once, Andrea saw Roger giggling with a female church member, touching her with familiarity. She had seen him standing with young, attractive women, their heads close together, their voices whispering in intimate conversation. More than once she had heard young women make comments about Roger that indicated they had a very close relationship—an inappropriately close relationship. She heard them make comments about his sexual relationship with his wife. "These things hinted at a level of intimacy that wasn't quite right, but I just couldn't believe it of Roger," Andrea said. "I wouldn't let myself believe it."

And so she dismissed the incidents as adolescent behavior, more indicative of the young women's level of maturity than Roger's character, and she concentrated on doing all she could to contribute to her church's ministry.

When some minor problems arose in Andrea's family, she went to Roger for counsel. Expecting him to encourage her and pray with her, she was surprised and hurt when he began criticizing her husband, making comments she later learned were lies. She left the session feeling troubled, confused, uneasy.

He's inexperienced at counseling, she thought. *He's young. He has a lot to learn.*

Her uneasiness grew when she heard Roger talk unkindly about fellow members of their church. And when he used Sunday morning sermons to scold people by name in front of the congregation, Andrea's distress increased. Roger's messages, once filled with encouragement and the loving, powerful thoughts of God, became more abusive than en-lightening.

Something was wrong, but Andrea didn't know what. Her uneasiness increased when Mrs. Sims, co-teacher of the women's class, left the church suddenly and without explanation. Feeling abandoned, Andrea was even more upset when Mrs. Sims rejected Andrea's efforts to communicate with her. But Andrea continued teaching, doing the work of two people, and tried to dismiss growing concerns for her church and its young pastor.

A Leader Struggles to Survive

In the final weeks before Roger's promiscuity was revealed, rumors about his sexual conduct began to circulate, but Andrea was left out of the grapevine. She knew only that Roger had begun telling various members of the church that he felt unappreciated, unloved, and overworked.

The truth was that when he learned of the rumors circulating about him, Roger began to fear for his job. He responded to the pressure of mounting criticism by subtly exerting pressure of another kind. He got word to his most loyal members that he felt mistreated, misunderstood. Maybe he should just resign.

Roger watched as his faithful, manipulated members responded exactly as he had predicted they would. They felt guilty. They had to do something to make their hurting pastor feel better. After all, it was their fault he didn't feel loved. It was their fault he was so tired and overworked. They couldn't let him resign.

Led by the older women of the congregation

who adored Roger, the company of the guilt-ridden organized a letter-writing campaign. They asked every member to write a note to the pastor, expressing love and appreciation for him. They planned a Saturday morning breakfast for Roger during which all the members would come and present their letters, making it a barrage of love and support for the weary pastor.

When Andrea was called and told about the plan, she was furious.

"I didn't want to write a letter to Roger," she said. "I couldn't understand how he could even think of leaving his congregation."

Andrea hadn't heard the secrets. She hadn't yet heard the stories. Stories that Mrs. Sims had taken with her when she left the church; stories about Roger's sexual involvement with a young woman in her Sunday school class; stories that Roger and his staff administrator had not denied.

Andrea had nothing more than a nagging sense of uneasiness and a conviction that Roger was wrong to consider leaving his church. It was involved in many meaningful and effective ministries—most of which he had initiated. How could he abandon this work? How could he abandon these people?

Struggling With the Truth

Andrea believed the church needed Roger. Yes, she sensed there were problems in his ministry, but at that time she had no idea how serious they were. Yes, she had been bothered by some unnamed, almost indiscernible questions about Roger, but she still believed he was God's man, doing God's work among this congregation and within the community. After all, the church was thriving. Good things were happening. Throughout many parts of the country, this church was touted as visionary, a model to be emulated wherever the church was serious about exploring and promoting creative ministries. And because it is our natural tendency to view any kind of success as evidence of God's blessing, it never occurred to Andrea that her pastor was involved in deliberate, gross sin.

Andrea, along with most of the members of the church, believed that if Roger left them, the ministry would suffer. They would suffer. They had no idea of the extent of suffering that awaited them in the upcoming weeks.

Soon after the Saturday breakfast (which Andrea refused to attend), Andrea heard the rumors of Roger's sexual behavior. Names were mentioned; situations of promiscuity were revealed; events detailed. But Roger made no definitive statement. The members of his church gathered to address the matter and, stunned and angered, they withdrew into separate camps. As usually happens, some members stood with the pastor, refusing to believe the charges against him. Others stood against him, anxious to rid their pulpit of his vile presence.

Leaders from a denomination that had been closely associated with Roger entered the scene, bringing their advice and encouraging the membership to oust him. Roger did indeed resign, and about a hundred and fifty members left with him to start a new church. Andrea was in the crowd a week later when he preached his next sermon in a small, rented office at a nearby shopping strip.

Some of those who followed Roger to his next

pulpit were certain that he had been falsely accused. That he had been wronged. But Andrea was not one of those. Reluctantly, sadly, she accepted that Roger had betrayed the trust of his congregation and his family. The subtle signs she had tried to ignore in earlier months now glared like lighted billboards. She had no doubt that he was guilty of sexual misconduct, but she also had no doubt that he was deeply contrite. She couldn't just walk away and leave him alone with the spiritual warfare she believed he was facing.

"I wanted desperately to see him be okay," Andrea said. "I believed he was a Christian. He was talented, gifted. I thought he was in the grip of demonic forces, and if all the Christians deserted him, he would have no chance of defeating Satan.

"I felt prayer could help deliver him, and I needed to be a part of that spiritual effort. With a body behind him, praying for his deliverance, I believed he could have a renewed ministry," she said.

"I was certain that, with prayer and support, he could begin again and build something worthwhile for the kingdom of God."

Believing the Signs

But Andrea's hope for Roger lasted about as long as it took him to get a new phone listing. As soon as he had his touch-tone, he was once again reaching out to women other than his wife. At first, Andrea was aware only of his lies.

"I caught him in lies, little lies that were unnecessary. You know, lying disorients us, it makes us feel crazy!"

But because she cared deeply for him, Andrea

continued to pray for Roger and treat him with patience, expecting every day to see signs that he was growing and maturing and gaining spiritual strength.

"I stayed with him at his new ministry for several months, hoping to see changes," Andrea said, "but they never came."

Rumors about Roger's moral life surfaced again within a short time. He denied them and viciously attacked his accusers. While he continued to preach to a small congregation that called itself "Grace Church," his wife filed for divorce.

Accusations and sordid stories continued to swirl around Roger. Little by little, his followers drifted away. Only a handful stayed with him, asking, "Where else can we go?" But this time Andrea was not among them.

"This time I knew I had to leave," she said. "I knew I would be all right. I would continue to trust God and He would minister to me, but that wasn't true for many of the people who were under Roger's ministry. Many of them won't go to church anywhere anymore."

God's People to the Rescue

In the wake of Roger's fall, Andrea was not without injury. Shortly after she left his tattered congregation, she sank into a deep depression that lasted nearly six months. Illness, her own as well as her husband's, complicated her emotional and spiritual condition, making church attendance impossible. Isolated from the friends who had been a vital part of her life, she had no church family to turn to for support.

It was during this long period when she was church-less that Andrea began hearing from old friends, Christian friends she hadn't seen or heard from in years. Often she picked up the phone to hear a familiar voice say, "You've been on my mind. I'm praying for you."

Cards and letters from believers prompted by the Holy Spirit encouraged Andrea and kept her feeling as though the arms of God were around her.

Though separated from a local body of believers—a church with a nearby street address and a membership roll on paper—individual members of the body of Christ reached out. Like the fingers of the hand massaging an aching limb, the body of Christ offered relief to a hurting member.

One Saturday morning, after nearly half a year of depression, Andrea answered her front door bell and found a handful of strangers on her front steps.

"They were a visitation team from my old church—where I had first met Roger and where I had taught the women's class. They invited me to come worship with them."

While they were talking, other members of the team walked up. Andrea recognized them as members who had stayed behind when she had left to follow Roger to his "church" in the shopping strip. These had stayed with the building and called an interim pastor after Roger's departure.

It might have been an awkward meeting—one who had supported the errant pastor versus those who had ousted him. In almost every case of this type, the congregation is divided and many members are filled with anger, sorrow, and bitterness toward one another. But there on Andrea's doorstep, instead of a stand-off, it was a celebration—a sort of family reunion, complete with hugging and weeping and laughter.

"They just pulled me into their arms and showed me such love!" Andrea said.

The next Sunday Andrea was back in church, wooed there by the love of the body. But it is a different body than before its leader fell. The large building that once housed nearly a thousand people is now home to a tiny group of Asian Christians. They worship there on Sunday mornings, filling a few pews in the front of the sanctuary. On Sunday afternoons, the remnant of Roger's congregation, those who ousted him, meets in another part of the building. On Sunday nights, they gather in a home for prayer and fellowship. They have only recently begun to venture out into the community, as they used to do, to invite newcomers to worship with them. For several months, they had been consumed with the business of binding their own wounds, tending to their own injuries, and waiting for God to heal. They had not had the time or energy to plan ministry expeditions into the lost community.

———

Sin has consequences. It sends chaos and confusion into the lives of God's children. It scatters His sheep. In a matter of days, hours, it can tear down a ministry that was carefully and prayerfully built over many years.

At one busy intersection in a huge bustling city is a parking lot that bears silent witness to that fact.

4

Voices of Leadership

The Storm Hits

"You could hear the tornado coming in the door."

Michael Griffen's voice rose an octave as the whites of his eyes assumed Little Orphan Annie proportions.

"It was like walking right smack into a tornado and watching everything fly," he said. "People wanted to know who knew what, and who didn't, and who knew but didn't say anything."

Usually every inch the dignified, unflappable seminary professor, Griffen was rocking on his chair, bouncing his outstretched arms, thoroughly enmeshed in his retelling of a recent difficult experience.

Michael Griffen had indeed walked into a tornado, as he had many times during the past twenty years. Widely recognized as a biblical history scholar, Griffen was fast becoming equally well-known as a type of pastoral 911—a capable pastor/leader willing to fill pulpits left suddenly vacant by fallen clergy. For him, emergency phone calls at odd hours usually meant an immediately full schedule of speaking responsibilities and volatile board meetings.

"Picture a tornado's destruction," Griffen explained. "Whatever's directly in its path will end up shattered, except for the single piece of china, the occasional door left on its jamb. It really doesn't matter which house is taller, which car heavier. As long as it's in the path, it goes. And when a church experiences a pastor's immorality, it's for certain the tornado's coming through the door."

In this chapter you'll meet three leaders who walked into the tornado's path and viewed its awful destruction. First, there's Michael Griffen, who knew to begin praying for wisdom the minute he would pick up the phone and hear the words, "We need you." Then, there's Walter Prescott, a minister of education serving in a megachurch when the founding pastor admitted to adultery. And last, you'll meet Timothy Sutton, who witnessed the fall of a much loved and respected fellow pastor, and walked him through the process of discipline and restoration.

God's Mediator

Michael Griffen's latest 911 came as a conference call, joining him with a Christian education minister, a music minister, and the head of a deacon board. Days earlier their long-time pastor had been accused of committing adultery with a woman in the church. By the time they called, the story had grown to include a long list of sexual offenses. By a majority vote of the board, the pastor had been immediately dismissed, with the provision that his salary be continued for three months.

Griffen walked into this scenario as a mediator in the truest sense. He had deacons so hurt and angry, so defensive and embarrassed, that they literally could not speak to each other. Yet he entered the fracas believing that this body must be healed. He likened it to a human body after surgery, where any more cutting would induce trauma certain to result in a fatality.

"At first I didn't know what kind of spiritual base to expect," Griffen said. "Often being an interim means preaching for months to a group of zombies." But when he examined the rubble he discovered two things: a humble dedication to prayer and a supportive foundation of trust.

First, he found Christians driven to their knees in prayer and deep contrition. Daily, beginning in early morning darkness, believers came together to unite in prayer at the church. In homes, in businesses, wherever members met, they joined in prayer.

Second, this church had been blessed with excellent leadership in many staff positions, and particularly in two: the minister of education and the minister of music. "When a leader falls, the character of all those closest to him also face examination, and the godly characters of both of these men remained intact. Their congregation possessed a huge amount of confidence and trust in them," Griffen said.

Through the healing of music, this splintered body still managed to unite in worship, led by the example of one who continued to praise God through his own time of mourning. And through the education ministry, individual Sunday school leaders were encouraged to function as pastors within their small groups, where trust and respect, already well established, could be nourished and encouraged to grow.

Yet even with the help of stable leadership and an uninterrupted schedule of services, Griffen wasn't sure that this church could survive. His doubts were fueled by events that happened one Sunday morning.

Taking the Reins

"It was right at the start of the 9:30 service as the organist was finishing his prelude. We were just starting to walk in when we got word of impending disaster," Griffen explained. "Some sort of lobby had positioned itself at each door of the sanctuary. People were passing out fliers along with the bulletins."

"It's a bunch of the ladies. Do you want us to stop them?" a young usher asked in a panic.

Griffen imagined the pandemonium that would cause. "No, sir, don't bother the ladies. Just get me a copy of what's being passed out."

The usher brought one to him, and there in black and white Griffen saw a list of all staff positions and salaries. To ease a depleted budget through uncertain times, the business committee had dismissed ten staff members (four of whom had been called by the church) without taking a vote of the congregation. Outrage over the seemingly too-high salaries of some, the continued salary to the former pastor, and the firings of key personnel had prompted these women, whose emotions were already overworked and whose frustrations were exaggerated by their perceived lack of power, to demand a few answers and to get some attention. They wanted the body to be informed. Although their motives were understandable, their methods appeared to Griffen to be disruptive and potentially damaging.

So what does the substitute pastor do to achieve some sense of oneness with the populace and still exercise a measure of authority and control? How can he be fair and listen to everyone, while at the same time keep discussions to a minimum?

Griffen and the others filed quickly onto the platform, he with the flier in hand. He moved to the pulpit and said, "My friends, please, let's not do church this way. We'll listen to your concerns, we'll give you a forum, but we really cannot worship like this." Fiercely protective of the worship service—a precious time for healing, for focusing together on the Lord rather than on the turmoil, and the body's only hope for being united—Griffen refused to allow it to be threatened.

"That's the day I really felt I began to pastor those people," he said. And Griffen continued in that capacity until the new pastor arrived several months later. He oversaw the re-hiring of many of the staff, and there was no further distribution of fliers.

Helping Them to See the Trap

As both an interim pastor and a seminary professor, Griffen sees the traps waiting for young men entering the ministry, and he takes every opportunity to voice his concerns. But he finds it difficult to convince idealistic young men of the dangers inherent in people-helping professions. "Zealous young seminarians come to us from a sexual culture where they are far more brainwashed than they can imagine," he says.

Our cultural triumvirate—money, power, and sex—gets mingled in their psyches along with pop psychology/self and biblical authority/God. Add to that the fact that young leaders starting out in small churches quickly learn to adopt the CEO mentality. They mold themselves after the pastor with the large church, hungry for God's perceived stamp of blessing, the success of numbers.

Though seminarians are repeatedly warned of the seductive dangers of money and power and position, those warnings come at a time when these earnest young men are on the bottom both socially and financially. Their marriages are new and fresh—two equal partners, young and in love, struggling to support each other, eyes filled with visions and ideals. The professor's nebulous warnings have no reality base in their minds. And if God does someday reward them with a measure of success, they have little doubt that they will possess the spiritual maturity to handle it.

Serving With the Vibrant Leader

Walter Prescott served under a pastor who began his ministry with high ideals. A man who was willing to roll up his shirt-sleeves. Young and fervent, fueled with vision, Pastor Rick stood looking at what to everyone else was an empty corner lot. But he saw a magnificent structure with parking garages filled to capacity and people streaming in from every surrounding neighborhood, people drawn to worship from all across this well-populated, up-scale, spiritually hungry metropolitan area. It was a vision that sent him canvassing neighborhoods and knocking on doors. It was a vision that kept him going through months of sparsely attended services in a nearby high school gym. And it was a vision that lit a fire in Walter Prescott's soul. He was one of the first to join Rick's team. Totally committed to seeing the dream realized, he was deeply grateful to be part of such a grass-roots, Spirit-led, enormously exciting ministry.

Prescott signed on as Pastor Rick's minister of education. Though older in years and experience, he possessed deep respect for this younger man who was so obviously led by God's hand.

It wasn't long before the vision began turning into reality. Visitation continued, large numbers responded, and wealthy patrons wrote checks for the property, the architects, and the pews. God's "new mercies every morning" became visible progressions toward a once seemingly impossible goal— daily visual reassurances of God's direction and blessing.

Within a few years a huge church did fill that corner, and people streamed in to pack multiple Sunday services. Ministries were established for seniors and singles, for the handicapped and the poor, and soon Sunday school attendance numbered in the thousands.

To have such a magnificent work stem from one man's vision and leadership most certainly guaranteed that man a huge amount of authority and respect.

"To the staff, Pastor Rick was 'The Boss,' " said Prescott. "He had made a lot of right calls, so we went on letting him make more. I'd never known anyone with such enormous creative energy. We couldn't help but elevate the man—we had *so much* trust in him."

A Church's Worst Nightmare

And then came the first accusation of an affair. One by one, key staff members learned of the woman's charges and began grappling with what should be done. Get more facts? Verify the story? Confront the pastor immediately, one on one? Go in pairs?

The morning the rumors started, nearly one hundred staff members met for a going-away party for one of the secretaries. Lots of tears were shed at that gathering, especially by Pastor Rick, which appeared to be a touching display of sadness over the loss of one of their "family." As Prescott watched the drama before him and struggled to reconcile recent sickening accusations with the empathetic leader he thought he knew, he couldn't shake the feeling that, very soon, most of those present would be out of work.

After the party, Pastor Rick followed Prescott into his office, wanting to know what he had heard. Before the conversation ended, he had confessed to having had "just two" affairs. Faced with the truth, having all doubts erased, Prescott urged the troubled leader to immediately tell the board everything.

The nine-member deacon board decided that Pastor Rick had to step down from his ministry. At first he refused to resign, causing them to begin dividing into enemy camps. Those supporting Rick excused him as overworked and vulnerable and called for a polling of the entire congregation. Letters addressed to the board were so hateful that Prescott felt sorry when secretaries had to read them. One letter read, "Every brick on this building is here because of Pastor Rick. I hope the woman who tricked him fries in hell."

The staff clung together for support, meeting at five every morning for prayer, even though some were working at the church until long after midnight. "We were heartbroken and we were angry," Prescott said. "We had worked long and hard, and now we could feel it all crumbling around our necks. So many people were getting beat up for nothing—his family, his wife, the deacons, the personnel committee."

Then came the announcement that Pastor Rick was moving on to start a new work, taking with him many of the church's well-to-do supporters, those who had latched onto Rick's powerful ministry and showered him with such gifts as cars and ski trips. But on the day Rick was scheduled to publicly announce his new work, news broke city-wide of multiple past affairs, ensuring that for Rick there would be no new pulpit ministry anytime soon.

It's All Over—Or Is It?

In Prescott's mind, his job was over. The pastoral search committee had formed, and he had to face two possibilities: First, the new pastor could come with his own education minister in tow; or second, that during this uneasy interim he could be called on to make difficult decisions that might render future ministry ineffective with some members of the congregation.

Once the pastoral search committee was

formed, the members spent the first six weeks simply meeting for prayer. When they finally did begin their search, God led them to a man strongly dedicated to preaching the Word, a man whose heart God had already prepared to lead them.

The church survived, the new pastor came, and Walter Prescott still serves as the minister of education. But he's no longer the same man. For him, the experience bounced him like a pinball from shock to sorrow to grief to anger to distrust. "For two years," he said, "not a day went by that I didn't wake up thinking about Rick, or go to bed without thinking about Rick."

When Repentance Is Real

Timothy Sutton, a long-time pastor whose own ministry remains scandal-free, was called on by his friend, a respected Christian leader, to lead him through a process of discipline and restoration after a fall.

Having been the pastor of a neighboring congregation, this brother had been well known to Sutton and the elders of his church for many years. Even after he left the area church and went to work for an evangelistic ministry, the leaders in Sutton's church remained aware of the man's work and whereabouts. So when these elders got wind of circulating rumors, they went straight to their brother, who immediately broke down and admitted to having had an affair.

Within days his ties to the evangelistic association were severed, and he sought out Sutton and the elders of his church for counsel and reconciliation within their church.

"When he first came to us we had no pattern to follow, no time limits established, no precedent for such a difficult task," Sutton said.

Though technically not a member of their church, this brother found in them a group of godly elders willing to assume the awesome responsibility of walking him through the process of restoration, a process new to everyone involved.

In many of the cases we have cited, the errant pastor eventually goes his own way, lost to the body, a statistic in the column marked "fallen." This story is important because it is one of a handful marked "restored." It's about a church that learned the process of healing as it walked a brother through, and about a hurting believer who experienced both spiritual and emotional restoration. A brother not lost to the body, but vitally precious to the church. A brother who was loved and led back into full fellowship.

"You'll never find anyone, anywhere, more genuinely repentant over his sin than this brother was," said Sutton. "He didn't come to us because he had hopes of getting a job back, or because a TV ministry was threatened. He came out of deep remorse and a sincere need for repentance and healing."

Sutton began the process by leading his elders through a study of Galatians 6, which begins with the words, "If someone is caught in a sin, you who are spiritual should restore him gently." Restore him, as you would set broken bones until they once more can function; as you would mend torn nets until they are strong enough to hold fish. Make him whole again. Bring him back.

The next step was to set up a committee of three elders to function as the restoration committee. Sutton saw these appointments as crucial to success. For an as-yet unspecified time these men would have authority over all areas of this brother's life. Submission was paramount to success, and, Sutton explained, such submission can happen only when an extremely mature and godly committee is in place, one made up of people the fallen pastor respects. "If that respect doesn't exist, if that pastor is too big in his own mind, then he can never submit to the discipline and accountability necessary for restoration," Sutton said.

The responsibility placed on the shoulders of these men was heavy. So many specifics had to be decided; so much wisdom was needed. What evidences of spiritual healing should they be looking for in the life of this man, or in his family? How often should meetings be scheduled, and in what areas and to what extent should he be made accountable? What, if anything, should be reported to the church at large? What counseling was needed? What was available? What restitution would be necessary? How could the spouse's needs be met? Should women be appointed to minister to her unique concerns? What criteria must be met before this man could officially be deemed "restored," and in what positions should he be allowed to minister in the future?

Is Full Restoration Possible?

Here is the question of restoration: Do we believe in members being restored to the body in full fellowship? Yes. Do we believe in leaders being restored to former positions of leadership? Maybe, maybe not.

"When it comes to restoration in the ministry, the church often either refuses to go through it at all or rushes through it much too quickly," said Sutton. "On one hand we've got those teaching that no one can ever return to ministry after moral failure, and we've got many on the other hand who are anxious to keep their highly visible, popular pastor in the pulpit regardless, without letting him miss a Sunday. Either we tend to restore our pastors badly, or we refuse to attempt it at all."

He continued, "In this brother's case, he gave evidence of genuine repentance, of a right relationship with God and with his family, and he preached a clear message of hope and healing. He willingly submitted to the church's authority, withdrew from public ministry and responsibility, confessed and sought to make restitution, and made himself accountable to others. After witnessing this evidence over a period of months, we, as elders, believing ourselves to be dependent on and sensitive to the leading of the Holy Spirit, unanimously voted to restore him to the ministry."

Here is where this committee assumed its heaviest burden of responsibility. Often when a pastor is caught in sexual sin, the church ships him off anywhere as quickly as possible, to disassociate themselves from public humiliation. But true restoration can only be accomplished when godly Christians personally assume responsibility for the healing and for the ministry of their fallen brother.

"The church that does the disciplining must take the risk," said Sutton. "They must keep him within their own congregation, and entrust him with specific ministry within that body. If they don't, if they send him somewhere else to heal and begin anew, he'll end up being killed one of three ways: either by gossip, or by repeating the sin, or by dying financially while he's waiting for a job."

Obviously there are specifics missing in this scenario. How long does the brother minister within that protected environment before being allowed to venture out on his own? What if, after a certain amount of time, that brother feels the need to come out from under that submissive relationship, even though the elders might disapprove? And if he cannot assume a ministry while he's healing in the church, is the church then responsible to provide him with other means of employment, or with financial support for his family?

These are tough questions for which there are no set answers that apply to every situation. Yet how exciting it is to see a body of believers working through them together, assuming responsibility for one another, and loving each other in practical ways through difficult times.

When faced with a pastor's fall into sexual sin the initial, instinctive response is to ship him down the road. But what a privilege it must be instead to become part of a brother's or a sister's spiritual healing and restoration. What a joy to follow the apostle Paul's example: "I do not frustrate the grace of God, for if righteousness could be gained by the law, Christ died for nothing" (Galatians 2:21).

Is it possible that we have seen so many Christian leaders fall, seen so many enslaved by sin and lack of repentance, that we've forgotten the restorative power of the grace of God? That by not expecting to see the grace of God in another's life, we may actually frustrate the working out of that grace? Are we seeing more and more failure because we're expecting less and less victory?

5

A Little Bit of Leaven

Who Is Your Role Model?

You are eleven years old and you've just gotten off the church bus after your first week of camp. Sticky, exhausted, and with pillow in one hand and licorice in the other, you make your way toward those to whom you want to say a last good-bye before your parents take you home. You walk right past the camp director; you stop and shake hands with the speaker; but then you spot your counselor, Miss Betty, the one who helped you clean the spilled shampoo out of your suitcase, the one who sensed how far away home seemed to you and whispered one last good-night in your ear after lights out, the one who missed skits on Thursday night to sit by the lake with you as you struggled under spiritual conviction. Although Miss Betty was not the camp pastor, she had certainly been God's minister to you for those six days.

You are twenty-one years old and you're in love. "Yes, yes, Lord! This is the one! I know we're ready!" You mustered up the courage to propose and she said yes. Forever's just beginning and it's looking mighty good. Who is the first person you'll break the news to at church? The pastor who preaches each week or the seminary intern who has led your singles group for the past two years and watched as your attraction for each other grew into love? The one who prayed with you in your commitment to purity? The leader you now want to perform your wedding ceremony, the one who has earned the privilege of uniting you before the Lord?

You are thirty-nine and shattered. Your teenage daughter has packed her things and stormed out in rebellion. You don't know where she's headed; you're not sure who her friends are; and for the first time in her life you have absolutely no control over it. You've given her over to the Lord many times, but her eyes are blind to spiritual truth; her heart is cold. And yours is broken. So who do you call in your distress? Do you dial the church phone number and ask if you can have a 2:00 appointment with the pastor on Tuesday? Or do you call your Bible study leader—the woman who for many months has led you through Psalms and First Peter, who has struggled with you to interpret your day-to-day life in the light of Scripture. Who knows you better? Which relationship is closer?

Are Pastors the Only Ones to Fall?

We have been focusing our attention on the moral failure of pastors, but is that entirely fair? Are pastors expected to possess a higher moral character than others within the body? In one sense, no. We are each called to moral purity. But in another sense, pastors are expected to be the very highest examples of moral purity within the church. As visible, recognized leaders, they are often more closely and more immediately identified as ambassadors and representatives of Christ to the masses. While the consequences of a pastor's moral failure may not be any more *serious* than that of a layperson's, they are certainly more far-reaching.

Yet within the body of Christ, many of us function as a leader to someone. Many lay leaders serve in positions of responsibility and authority. While not as powerful or as visible as the head pastor, these leaders often touch more lives more closely than does the pastor himself. The closest bonds form in the smallest groups, not in the sanctuary.

Within our own specialized units—the choir, the visitation teams, the youth group, the singles class, whatever—we find our identity, and we relate to that particular teacher or director or leader as our pastor in the more immediate, practical sense. Our identity within the church body is defined by whatever special interest group we most closely align with. If the leader of one group falls, fewer people are wounded than when a senior pastor falls, but the injuries to those hurt by the fall of a small group leader can be deeper and more damaging.

Whether we are camp counselors, Bible study teachers, or choir directors, we are in a capacity of leadership. Whether we host a radio program, travel the country as an evangelist, or head a parachurch ministry we are looked up to as role models. Whether we minister to youth, to singles, to seniors, we must set the example. Maybe we serve simply as leaders in our own families.

A Marriage Made in Heaven?

Denise and Greg met in their seventh grade math class, and he was "the cutest thing" she'd ever seen. During their senior year they began dating seriously, and that was also the year when Denise accepted Christ. "Greg and I had grown up in church together," she said. "He had been a Christian since he was a little boy, but I didn't make a commitment to Jesus Christ until I was eighteen. It was a dramatic moment in my life, a very powerful event."

Denise and Greg dated throughout that year and graduated together in the early sixties. They married one year later. They had common goals, common values, and similar family backgrounds— all the things necessary to create a foundation for a strong, lasting marriage.

Their relationship was like most Christian marriages at that time—she a stay-at-home mom and he inching toward success on the corporate ladder. Early on they established the habit of regular church attendance. Soon Greg's musical talents were recognized within the church, and eventually he accepted the position of lay minister of music. The church became the focus of Greg and Denise's family life, and whenever the doors were open Greg insisted the family be present.

In the late seventies, when the youngest of their four children started school, Denise began asking God how she could use her extra time for ministry. God led her into a women's Bible study group, and soon she was asked to train for a leadership position. Before long she was standing before huge groups of women teaching the Bible.

She thrived, he thrived, and things were on track. They had a nice house, good kids, and a solid marriage.

Then came the year everything changed.

Denise knew Greg was troubled. He had formed a partnership and started a new business, but had been stunned at not being chosen company president. He fought depression, and for the first time in their marriage Denise and Greg were unable to talk. Yet it never occurred to Denise that his pressures were related to anything other than business.

One night Greg finally had something to say. While driving home after a visit with friends, Greg told Denise, without preamble, that he wanted a divorce. He said he would not see a counselor and assured Denise that the kids, who were almost grown, would be okay.

"Nothing about that night seemed real," Denise said. By the time they reached home she was ill. She had all the physical symptoms of shock. She was nauseous and sweating, and her chest ached with every breath; she felt as if she were having a heart attack.

Greg, on the other hand, went right to bed and slept through the night. He got up the next morning, asked where breakfast was, and went off to church, surprised when she chose to stay home.

"I sat before the Lord all that week, praying and asking God what to do," she said. "And there came a point, while I was praying, that I sensed the finality of it all. I knew Greg was leaving and my marriage was over."

Within weeks Greg moved away, leaving his home, his family, his church, and his twenty-plus-year marriage. At the time Denise had no reason to suspect adultery, but she soon found evidence that Greg had been having an affair. Within a few months of their divorce he was remarried.

No Simple Solutions

When Greg ended his marriage to Denise, he also ended his ministry. But his ministry wasn't the only one lost in his fall. Denise lost hers as well. Divorce immediately disqualified her as a leader/teacher within the organization she had so grown to love.

"I wanted to die during that first year," Denise said. "I really did. I prayed I would die. The hurt of that year was awful. And because all these women had looked up to me, they too were hurt. Regardless of whose fault a divorce is, people are going to be damaged."

Denise knew how uncomfortable she made her friends feel. People wanted reasons, they needed to cast blame to assure themselves that their own marriages were less vulnerable to failure. She sat alone in the pew Sunday after Sunday. Others actually got up and moved one time when she sat beside them.

"There is pride within the church," Denise explained. "Without uttering a word, Christians say to the divorced person, 'I am better than you because it happened to you and not to me.' It's like getting mugged twice. When I call you and say I was mugged, you say how awful! Then the next day you ask what I was doing out alone at night."

Although Denise had long been surrounded and supported by a huge circle of Christian friends, she went through her grief very much alone. "My friends wouldn't let me talk about my grief and anger. The church doesn't deal well with grief. I wasn't supposed to be sad, but to just get on with my life. Friends would see me in the grocery store and ask how I was doing, and I'd think, 'If you pick the grocery store to ask me then you really don't want to know.' " Denise the care-giver was needing some care, and her friends couldn't accept her in that position. They couldn't reverse the roles.

One fall into sin, two ministries ended, and gaping needs left unmet by a dysfunctional body.

"Divorce is a dilemma, meaning there's no *good* answer for it," Denise explained. "Either way you go isn't perfect. Everybody loses. Yet in Scripture whenever God's people encountered a dilemma, God provided deliverance. And for me, *He* was my deliverance. He was there when others weren't."

Today Denise teaches singles' Bible studies in various churches throughout her city, bringing to each the thorough preparation she learned during her many years in leadership. She also brings the sensitive heart of one who can understand and empathize with that often misunderstood group, the newly divorced Christians.

While at least two ministries were destroyed as the result of Greg's fall, God has graced Denise with healing, humor, wisdom, and continued opportunities for ministry. Yet the repercussions of that fall reached beyond their immediate family, beyond their local church, and far out into the Christian community at large.

It's Hard to See Through a Natural Talent

Jared was a shining star. The darling of his denomination. He could captivate an audience with a voice one writer likened to the sound of a jackhammer pitched two octaves above middle C. Shrill and yet gravelly, its force and volume could pin listeners to a wall one minute, then abruptly soften to caress them into a warm circle of faith. Congregations across the nation wept with him, walked up aisles to stand and pray with him, and sent money to buy tapes of his sermons. And night after night those congregations asked, "When are you going to put your story into a book?"

As is common for many enjoying the limelight today, Jared decided to write the story of his life. Armed with taped sermons, videos, and a cache of childhood memoirs, Jared hired Dan, a Christian with other "as-told-to's" already under his belt, to co-author his book.

Whenever Jared was in town the two would meet to fill in details, verify names and places, and edit finished chapters. With impressive book sales virtually guaranteed due to Jared's full calendar of speaking engagements, publishers started to negotiate for the publishing rights before the book was half-finished.

And then something happened. One unsettling incident.

During a simple conversation between Dan and a woman visiting his church, Jared's name came up. The woman erupted in anger.

"He's a womanizer!" she said, shaking her head. "He was involved with two or three women in another church! He admitted it! I could never listen to him preach again! That man is a fake!"

Who to Believe?

In quiet horror Dan asked for facts—who, where, and how long ago. With list in hand, he determined to investigate the charges, going first to a leader in Jared's denomination, a man who had mentored the young preacher through his first pastorate as a Bible student. If what the woman had said was no more than a cruel rumor, this man would not repeat it and jeopardize Jared's ministry. He knew Jared well. If he could answer these allegations and testify to Jared's integrity, Dan could continue with the book project.

When questioned, this leader assured Dan that all rumors had been personally investigated and found to be untrue. "The whole thing was generated by jealousy. You know how women can be in a church. Jared is absolutely innocent of any wrongdoing."

Each of the accusers had been women; each had been interviewed separately; each had changed her story; each had a history of instability.

"Make no mistake, Jared used poor judgment. But what young pastor hasn't at one time or another? That doesn't make him immoral," the man told Dan.

Dan walked out of that office relieved. This reliable man knew Jared well, had personally investigated the rumors, and still believed in his innocence. Based on this information, Dan also believed in Jared's innocence. Further investigation seemed unnecessary. To ask more questions would only spread the damaging rumors. Instead, Dan continued his work on the book.

The Sham Uncovered

Three months later Jared's church charged him with sexual misconduct. Local newspapers ran stories of the rising young star's sudden crash. Jared resigned, his denomination denounced him, and his wife filed for divorce.

As an evangelist/preacher, Jared had filled pulpits across the country and had become a visible and dynamic leader within his denomination. Seldom did he preach before the same sea of faces more than two or three nights at a time. And now each of those faces wore a look of stunned disbelief. Although hundreds upon hundreds had never met Jared personally, they possessed a spiritual bond with him because they'd heard his power-packed preaching of God's Word.

Again, the victims were many.

First, the writer. Not a close friend, not a family member, but in essence a business associate. A partner in a project linking his name to Jared's. Using his time and skills to communicate what he believed was a truly remarkable story of God's grace, he came dangerously close to validating what turned out to be a lie, to connecting God's truth in one line to a man's contrived story in another. Lies juxtaposed to truth—God's truth; the creation of a false image. If the book had gone to print, Dan's credibility and integrity as a writer might have been forever compromised.

He had checked out Jared's story. He had quietly gone to a leader in authority and, in confidence, voiced his questions about Jared. Had he been lied to in some sort of cover-up, "for the sake of the ministry"?

Judge Not

Let's walk for a moment in the shoes of the man Dan trusted. He too had received "just enough" reassurances from other sources that the charges were false. Both men were in extremely vulnerable positions. While Dan's name had not yet been linked publicly to Jared's, this leader's had, and he now had to justify the part he had played in allowing Jared's ministry to continue.

How tremendously difficult it is for one believer to judge another in such a way that will threaten that person's work for the Lord. Can we ever be "sure enough" to blow the whistle, knowing what grave consequences await? Until a sin is proven to be true, until the rumors are substantiated, do we not rightfully struggle to believe the best of our brothers and sisters and to commit them to God's quiet discipline behind closed doors?

Yet as members of the body we are all in danger of being injured by a fellow believer's fall.

A music minister, a Bible teacher, an evangelist, a writer, a denominational head. All functioning, productive ministries either threatened or destroyed by a leader's fall. What happens to one part of the body affects many, if not all, of its members.

"Do you not know that a little leaven leavens the whole lump of dough?" (1 Corinthians 5:6, NASB).

If a pastor commits adultery, does his sin in any way expose those pastors under him to a greater risk of falling themselves? When a Bible teacher falls, are his or her students more susceptible? When a parent falls, are the children more vulnerable to their own immorality? Does sin really spread throughout the entire body once we let it in the door?

The Domino Effect

In the case of one church, the fall of the head pastor led to a domino-like toppling of three serving under his headship: a pastor to senior adults, a youth pastor, and a minister to the deaf. Within days of the head pastor's confession to an affair, his ministry at that church ended, and he immediately left to begin a new work elsewhere. While this example is in no way offered as a typical pattern to which all churches are susceptible, the fact that so many ministries within this one body ended due to charges of moral failure (and/or sexual impropriety) makes the issue of leaven-spreading inescapable.

This large church, with a heart for the physically challenged and the money available to fund special ministries, opened its doors to the deaf community by providing signed interpretations of its services. This soon led to an active group of twenty to thirty hearing-impaired individuals—some children, some adults, but most of them in their high school and college years. For these, the group provided a wonderful opportunity for fellowship, worship, and social gatherings, something difficult for them to find within the hearing world.

Before long the ministry grew to include Sunday school classes, weekend fellowship times, and a signing choir. A young, single seminary intern was hired to pastor the deaf. Though hearing, he knew how to sign, and though young enough to lead the kids, he was knowledgeable enough to teach the adults.

In time the group grew close to one another and developed a strong loyalty to and dependence upon their leader.

Occasionally one of the hearing parents would take part in an activity, and more than once these parents felt uneasy vibes. One parent learned that one of the girls did the leader's laundry. Another found out that one of the more needy members of the group gave the leader an expensive gift. And every so often this young leader would make sexual comments, quiet innuendoes under his breath, forgetting that a hearing person was present. Yet the group loved the leader, and he seemed to be serving them well.

After he had been with them for over a year, a woman from outside the church went to the elders with charges that this man had slept with her, promised to marry her, then dumped her. They called the man in and let him answer the charges. At first he denied everything the woman said, but eventually the lie grew too heavy to carry and he admitted to the truth. He was dismissed. Before this young man had even completed his education, he had taken a fall that would forever shadow his ministry.

Those with special needs are often the most dependent, and the deaf were deeply hurt by their leader's betrayal and abandonment. Spiritually, most of them were still babes, and they needed another pastor to help them through their trauma. While this large church still had plenty of pastors on staff, there were none with whom the deaf could communicate. Here was a group with little voice and no power, who had seen their haven of acceptance and fellowship threatened. Too often ostracized by the world, they were now being set apart even within the church. Imagine their sense of loss. Imagine how difficult it would be for them to trust their next minister and to develop a sense of love and loyalty for him.

A Common Bond Is Broken

The leader of the senior adults came to the church as a newly retired pastor. Possessing well-honed ministerial skills, he was much admired by the rest of the staff, and, sharing the same day-to-day concerns as those with whom he served, he was much loved by them.

A Sunday morning regular in the halls of the adult educational wing, he was quick with a hello and warm hug. For many elderly members who were far from their families, this was their haven and they eagerly waited to shake hands with the seniors' minister and hear a personal word of encouragement.

Then came the Sunday the church announced the adultery and subsequent dismissal of its founding pastor—a gifted, vibrant young man. To the senior adults, he had been like a son. They had prayed for his ministry. They had parented his wife and his children. To a group daily facing loss and last good-byes, the abrupt departure of someone so dear didn't fit. There had been no good-bye, no resolution.

Like those in the deaf congregation, these senior adults felt powerless. The elders left in charge of making crucial decisions were mostly their juniors. Numbed with shock, unnerved by sudden change and deep disappointment in a young man's failure, this group looked to their own leader for stability and direction.

But hardly had the young pastor left before their

own education corridor was empty. To an elder board battered and exhausted from handling one leader's fall, accusations of impropriety sent them scurrying to clean house. Charges brought against the senior adults' minister had been substantiated, and seemingly overnight he was gone. Too numb for anger, their emotions long spent, these older members felt only deep sorrow and multiple loss.

And it wasn't over. The pile of the wounded in that church just got bigger. Tragically, while this congregation struggled through the loss of their pastor and two associates, they were yet to face another leader's moral failure. The third associate minister to fall was the very popular, very talented, much loved assistant youth pastor.

Offending the "Little Ones"

All members are vulnerable, but perhaps none as much so as the children. Few groups within a church assign more loyalty to a leader than do the youth. And no group is more likely to be seriously affected by a trusted leader's fall into immorality. Sexual temptation is a struggle they themselves encounter daily, and they rightfully expect to have leaders who are committed to moral purity. Adolescents don't invest trust easily. While adults may be able to forgive one another for saying one thing and doing the opposite, youth cannot or do not. Adolescents don't accept hypocrisy. If one part of the message is a lie, the whole message becomes suspect.

Daily, in high school and college classrooms, these young minds are constantly being challenged to question matters of faith and morality that both parents and churches have worked hard to instill. Disillusioned by the moral failure they have witnessed, a protective wariness, even a cynicism, often threatens their ability to trust the next spiritual leader who enters their life with answers, who comes claiming to be a friend. Members of a youth group will suffer much deeper wounds from a youth leader's fall than from that of a head pastor.

To focus totally on the effects of a senior pastor's fall would leave unrecognized the serious damage done to the body when a leader in any position chooses to risk his or her ministry for the pleasure of a season of sin.

No matter how or in what capacity we serve the body, if we choose the path of adultery, unfaithfulness, or immorality, we will be responsible for inflicting deep wounds on the body of Christ, the church.

Part II

———

Choices

6

Choices From the Bottom of the Heap

What Constitutes Forgiveness?

After a Christian leader falls there are many choices to be made, beyond those left to the elders and deacons. The first choice is made by the adulterer himself. Will he repent and seek restoration, or will he continue his sinful behavior? The second choice is then left to the wife. Will she forgive him if he repents? Can she commit to the healing and restoration of her marriage and family? Or will she choose the biblical "exception clause," divorce him, and start a new life?

For Christians, forgiveness is not usually considered a matter of choice, yet true forgiveness does require an act of will. It takes willful determination to say, "What happened is past; I won't hold it against you. Starting today we enter a new relationship with each other."

When we choose to forgive, we choose to give up our right to repay wrong for wrong, hurt for hurt.

Some say that forgiving requires forgetting as well, but how can a wife, once betrayed, ignore warning bells when an inappropriate comment causes her to feel unsettled, or when an unexplained absence fuels her imagination? Would it even be wise to do so?

It is impossible to completely and instantly reestablish trust in a mate who has been unfaithful. Some doubts refuse to be silent. For a wife to choose forgiveness means simply that she is willing to begin a new relationship. It does not mean that she is willing to go on being ignorant and naive.

The rebuilding of trust and confidence takes time. Neither partner is going to reawaken to find things magically restored and healed. Yes, God does give grace, but it's a grace that empowers us to survive difficult times, not escape them.

Asking the Tough Questions

Before making a decision on whether or not to continue this marriage, the spouse must ask herself some difficult questions: Am I emotionally and psychologically strong enough to invest the time and energy necessary into starting over? Can I commit to months, maybe years, of doubts, confrontations, and total honesty? Is it wise to make myself and my children vulnerable to another trauma of this magnitude?

When a wife chooses to commit to the healing of her marriage, she exposes both herself and her family to the real possibility of the repeated pain of adultery. Yet, while such a commitment is a difficult choice to make, it is in fact a beautiful testimony of love and grace. Though wounded, she declares to her spouse:

I love you, and I believe our marriage is worth the sacrifice of putting your healing and restoration before my own needs at this time. Please recognize that I too am fragile. But I am choosing to be vulnerable once again. And though I love you deeply, I cannot promise that I will be able to repeat this commitment if in the future I'm again forced to experience such hurt and betrayal.

How wonderful to see the grace of God restore hearts and lives. How blessed we are that we *can* choose to make ourselves vulnerable to one another because we trust in an Almighty God and because we recognize what a privilege it is to have a life that testifies of His healing and grace.

As Christians we have a hope that is central to every decision we make. That hope, eternal and rooted in Christ, is God's assurance that our victory is certain. Believers will *never know* hopelessness. Even when we do not see the light, we have no doubt that it's there. And it's that hope that enables us to risk vulnerability.

Walking Together

Two people with renewed commitments to God and to each other *can* save their marriage. But it won't be easy.

Both partners are facing a life different from the one they planned for, dreamed of, and have known to this point. Both must be ready to make some substantial adjustments.

For the fallen leader, the memory of moral failure will be a constant reminder of his own weakness. For the spouse, it will be a constant reminder of her vulnerability. Both have suffered censure, loss of privacy, loss of position and ministry, loss of stature and respect. Both are wounded, confused, and uncertain.

While there exists no guarantee that another fall will not occur, there is a guarantee that healing and oneness are possible through the power of God's love. All any of us can be sure of is that God will honor our decisions to walk step by step in obedience to His will.

Forgiveness is not only the first step, it's also the most important one because it sets the direction for all future steps. Once the guilty spouse asks for forgiveness and the offended spouse forgives, the couple can move toward trust, intimacy, and respect. We suggest the following five steps for enabling that to happen.

1. *Commit to making the marriage a top priority.* Couples recovering from infidelity once stood before God and made promises to Him and to each other. Those first vows were broken. Now they need to be said again—by both partners. Not in some elaborate public display where their sincerity might be questioned, but privately, as two rejoined as one before God, putting the past behind and promising anew to love, honor, and cherish each other. They need to make their marriage, and therefore their mate, their top priority—before ego, before business, before outside responsibilities—and again pledge before God to be faithful to each other.

2. *Commit to honest communication.* It is imperative that each learn to communicate honest needs to the other. While trying to reestablish intimacy, an honest, open policy is the only one that will work in enabling them to reach their goal. If such open communication seems impossible at first, counseling is mandatory. A professional counselor is trained to help the silent partner speak and the more open partner listen.

A crucial part of honest communication is the injured spouse's freedom to voice her true feelings. Dr. Frank Pittman, in his book *Private Lies: Infidelity and the Betrayal of Intimacy*, recommends that she admit that she is "angry, upset, frightened, and insulted," and that she "express this fully, until it is perfectly clear to [her] unfaithful partner how much this has hurt [her]."[1]

Dave Carder in *Torn Asunder: Recovering From Extramarital Affairs* explains that "in most cases it will take the spouse as long to recover as it took the infidel to get into and out of the affair," and that "the closest thing to a guarantee that the infidel won't stray again is for him to feel fully the pain that he has caused the wounded spouse."[2]

It is not wrong to honestly express anger, hurt, and fear. Rather, honesty is imperative to healing.

3. *Commit to accountability.* Accountability isn't easy for anyone. We all resent questions, intrusions into our privacy, and easy advice. But in the event of a Christian leader's fall into adultery, some form of church discipline will need to be enforced. The spouse needs to understand what levels of accountability will be expected of her as well as of her husband, and what ministries she will be allowed to continue. Discipline is necessary for the healing of the body, but for a faithful spouse this will sometimes seem a bitter pill to swallow. It is, however, simply one more part of the process of healing and restoration.

Though difficult at times, accountability need

---

[1]Dr. Frank Pittman, *Private Lies: Infidelity and the Betrayal of Intimacy* (New York: Norton, 1989), p.155.
[2]Dave Carder with Duncan Jaenicke, *Torn Asunder: Recovering from Extramarital Affairs* (Chicago: Moody, 1992), pp. 114, 134.

not and should not be adversarial. In Chapter 4 we mentioned the importance of having a restoration committee made up of believers whom the fallen leader trusts and respects. It is also imperative that this committee includes at least one godly woman whom the spouse trusts and respects, someone to whom she can voice her needs and emotional struggles. If the spouse doesn't feel equally comfortable with this committee it likely will fail. Submission to this disciplinary body is paramount to success, and if respect doesn't exist, neither will submission.

Such submission won't be easy for either the husband or wife. It won't be pleasant to have to explain behaviors and decisions. But when a couple chooses the path of forgiveness and restoration, they are agreeing to forfeit some of their personal privacy and independence for the greater good, the greater healing.

Taking steps to heal a marriage is an act of will. Then eventually, as confidence and trust is gradually restored, fewer questions will be asked.

4. *Commit to healing the family.* Things can't continue as before. Huge changes may be necessary. A career change into a field offering less recognition and fewer accolades may be called for.

Changes in habit will be in order. The mandate to flee immorality must be seriously followed, governed by a renewed, healthy fear of sin's power and by the reality of one's own moral weaknesses. It may be necessary to avoid certain movies and TV programs, magazines and books. Make those changes. Both spouses must be willing to make sacrifices to protect the other from temptation. Those who assume they possess enough spiritual strength to handle sexual temptation are only increasing their risk of taking another fall.

5. *Commit to spiritual integrity.*

For the adulterer, this means that he now begins to live the life he has professed to be living.

For the spouse who has been wronged, spiritual integrity requires a refusal to punish. Writes Henry Virkler in *Broken Promises: Healing and Preventing Affairs in Christian Marriages*, "The faithful partner needs to recognize that, while the affair was wrong, it is just as much a sin to feed an unforgiving spirit as it is for one's mate to continue to nurture romantic feelings for another person."[3]

Forgiveness is neither easy nor instant, but refusing to avail one's self of the patience, gentleness, humility, and submission that makes forgiveness possible is in itself a very serious and damaging sin. While the acknowledgment of honest feelings of anger, betrayal, and hurt opens a very necessary door to healing, dwelling on such negatives only feeds them and encourages their growth. It renders intimacy impossible and guarantees a future marriage in name only, where the loneliness of both spouses deepens and the marriage becomes a tragic testimony of the failure to love.

How easy it is to fall. And how easily our lives can become testimonies of failure rather than trophies of God's grace and love. Yes, the adulterer is responsible for his choices, but the spouse is equally responsible for hers.

We in the body each bear the responsibility to flee immorality and keep ourselves pure. Full-blown adultery is not the only sexual sin that the Bible condemns. Some may be experts at hiding

---

[3]Henry A. Virkler, *Broken Promises: Healing and Preventing Affairs in Christian Marriages* (Dallas: Word, 1992), p. 216.

questionable magazines in a nightstand or sprin-
kling conversation with suggestive innuendoes.
Under the guise of friendship, counseling, or compassion some have allowed a degree of intimacy to
develop between themselves and someone other
than their spouse, and they are not willing to give
it up. Relationships are sometimes misrepresented
to others, even to ourselves, by defining them in
spiritual terms. Others have perfected a fantasy sex
life that isolates them from their spouse during
times of intimacy.

We in the body of Christ are called to lead lives
of moral purity in the midst of a disintegrating so-
ciety where sex is touted as the cure-all, where perceived needs take precedence over vows and commitments, and where "maturity" has come to mean
sympathizing with the adulterer. Our spiritual integrity is at stake.

The Christian ideal is for all relationships to be
healed and for all families to remain intact. But unfortunately that is not always possible. A woman
who may eventually be able to forgive her spouse's
adultery may be so physically, mentally, and emotionally spent at the time of the crisis that she is
simply too fragile to reenter their marital relationship. She may be incapable of continued vulnerability. Although God hates divorce, He allows it in
cases of adultery. Jesus made the exception clear:
no divorce "except for marital unfaithfulness" (Matthew 19:9).

Walking Alone

Whether the spouse wants out of the marriage
or the adulterer chooses sin over reconciliation, of-

ten adultery prefaces the breakup of a home and family, and leaves the spouse suddenly walking the single path.

Eventually divorce is mentioned, and for possibly the first time in either spouse's life comes the scramble to find a good lawyer.

Everything is up for grabs. Every last possession must be bartered for and divided—right down to the children (a sickening thought but true nonetheless—another blatant reminder of the tragedy of divorce). Divorce affects every aspect of life—the home, finances, possessions, warranties, insurance, taxes, jobs, future plans, ministries, relatives, friends. Everything. So the first thing the wife needs is good advice.

The task of choosing a lawyer and confronting a spouse may seem so daunting that she is tempted to let her husband take what he wants and make all the decisions. At a time when simply fixing dinner and chauffeuring children seems to demand every ounce of strength she has, finding the energy to undertake a legal battle while pursuing spiritual discernment may seem absolutely impossible.

At this point she needs to remember two things: first, for the sake of the children, she must take responsibility and exercise sound judgment; and second, the man she's dealing with now is not the same man she married.

In some cases, it may be possible for the couple to hire a Christian mediator and settle their divorce outside of court. This type of service can be beneficial for several reasons: (1) a mediator is able to listen to and protect both sides equally; (2) a mediator can instill calm and cooperation through impartiality; (3) the mediator will make suggestions but allow the couple to make final decisions; (4) the mediator costs a lot less money than two lawyers will cost.

Ending a marriage is not one single hurdle that has to be crossed before moving ahead; it's more like giving birth to a new life. And giving birth is not only painful, it often seems endless.

For the woman who realizes her marriage has ended, we offer the following advice:

1. *Seek professional financial advice.* Find a believer you can trust to keep things confidential and whose sound business reputation and integrity have been proven and remain intact. Request from that person a step-by-step plan by which you can reestablish financial control of your household. Do financially what you can when you can, and trust God to see that your needs are met.

2. *Seek emotional support from a spiritually mature friend.* Ask God to bring you at least one special friend for strength and support, a woman with whom you can pray and be honest. A woman of proven character, and one whose confidentiality you trust. A friend who is able to laugh and listen and cry and hug.

3. *Trust God to surround you with people who will help in your healing.* You will expect certain people to step forward in support, but in many cases you will be disappointed. Even in your disappointment, however, the Holy Spirit has not stopped moving. At this very moment, He is softening hearts and directing people your way. Be watchful, so that you will recognize them as His messengers to you. And remember that someday you will again be the one sent to others.

4. *Trust your instincts.* When you get a feeling

that something's not right, stop and think. When someone gives advice that doesn't make sense, investigate it, find out why. You are a responsible person, gradually regaining control of your life, and you owe it to yourself to pay attention to your instincts.

5. *Refocus your attention.* One way to more quickly achieve personal healing is to visually put yourself into the hands of God, leave the job of worrying over "you" to Him, and redirect your attention. A good place to start is with your children.

Most likely you will be the parent responsible for the day-to-day care of the children, which means that you will also be the one responsible for their emotional and psychological recovery. Your children are experiencing loss and separation, confusion and anxiety, sorrow and anger, that is comparable to your own. They too need help to find their way through the rubble. Here are some ways a mother can help.

1. *Remind them often of how much they are loved.* Children live a dependent existence, and to lose their father in this way is to lose their greatest source of security. They realize that if one parent can leave, so can the other. The parent who stays can't make everything right. She can't replace her children's sense of security by herself. But she can relieve some of their insecurity by taking every opportunity to remind them of her love, of their father's love, and of the Lord's love. It may be a long time before they *feel* loved, but the sound of her words and the sense of her touch will provide a growing measure of security. Their security must come from knowing that God is the parent who will *never* leave, and that their mother is the parent who

will never leave them by choice.

2. *Be honest.* For a mother to say everything's okay when it isn't will only increase her children's insecurity. They will sense the contradiction. Instead, admit that problems exist, and then assure them that God is bigger than those problems. On the other hand, remember that honesty doesn't necessitate overloading young minds with details they can't understand and emotions they can't handle. Let *them* ask the questions—*encourage* their questions—and then respond honestly and prayerfully.

It is a normal response for a loving, hurting parent to want to bury sorrow rather than admit it to the children. Unfortunately, when these children witness our denial of emotion, they conclude that they too must bury their own hurt. Honesty is a much healthier response to pain than stoicism. When sin occurs everyone who is wounded needs to mourn. Our tears are precious to God.

Among friends and perhaps even while visiting the other parent, children will quickly learn to mask their emotions, which is why they need home to be a place where absolute honesty is not only allowed but encouraged. Once at home, those masks need to come off at the door.

3. *Let them hear you laugh.* Laughter heals. It comforts young listeners, provides needed relief, and reminds everyone that there has been no ultimate defeat. There is still hope for a happy future.

4. *Don't let them feel guilty.* Children see from one perspective: their own. When they look for reasons for the breakup of the family, the only contributing factors they see clearly are those they themselves had a part in. They take everything personally. A hurting spouse knows firsthand the weight of car-

rying guilt for another's sin. Children carry that same type of false blame, guilt they were never intended to bear, guilt they are incapable of bearing. If left on their own to cope with this guilt, they may suffer emotional consequences for many years.

5. *Give them time and, if necessary, counseling.* Children are the innocent victims of adultery. To compensate for the "loss" of their father, they may demand huge amounts of attention from the mother. Sudden change and feelings of abandonment have interrupted their growth process. Instinctively, they will often regress, and return to behaviors emotionally connected to more secure times.

As much as a distraught parent needs her children to be well-behaved and understanding, she must realize the depth of their fear and anger, their sense of betrayal. Firmly but patiently she should do her best to help them work through the nightmares, the temper tantrums, the inability to concentrate at school, the fantasies, the uncharacteristic rebelliousness.

Children in their teens may heal the most slowly. They had started the process toward independence, of moving away from the family for short periods of time, venturing out into the world to test their strength, and then coming back to refuel (often literally). But now they have returned home to find their haven bombed and gutted. Mom is trying her best to put things back together, but she can't do it alone. She needs their help. Younger siblings need their help.

But they're not sure they *want* to help. They'd rather just flee the disaster site. Caught in that awkward period between childhood and adulthood, they see how others need them, but they still feel the need to be taken care of themselves.

Teens will generally respond in one of two ways, depending on the level of independence they've achieved. If they still feel more comfortable in the realm of childhood, they, like their younger siblings, will also regress, perhaps into adolescent rebellion or into refusing to leave the safety of the familiar. If on the other hand the realm of adulthood is more comfortable to them, they may rush back out into the world without taking time to refuel, assuming behaviors far more adult than they are emotionally ready to handle. While they certainly look mature and have learned to say things that make them sound mature, the truth is that their psychological development has been suddenly arrested by the destruction of their family.

On a Donahue show dealing with the children of parents who had committed adultery, one teenage girl sat on the platform answering questions from her sympathetic host and a supportive audience. Her father had left her mother for another woman. "But it's really okay," the girl said. "I understand that he needed to be happy, and I'm glad he's happy now. What happened really was no one's fault."

Her words and calm demeanor seemed to impress those listening. Her mature attitude amazed Donahue, who concluded that, with the right help, children can survive their parents' adultery and divorce without becoming bitter and disillusioned.

Yet one fact contradicted every word the girl said. As she spoke calmly to the audience that day, repeatedly claiming that everything was fine and that no one was to blame, tears streamed down her cheeks. Her counselors apparently had told her that mature people get past their hurt and assess no blame. Trying her hardest to believe them, she repeated what they said. But through her tears that young girl was telling the world that every word she said was a lie. Unfortunately, those listening seemed to hear only what they wanted to hear— that no one was to blame, that everything was fine.

Adding to the dilemma for adolescents is the sudden loss of ready cash at a time when the right clothes, shoes, and haircut, not to mention gas and a car, mean everything. Think too of their struggle to contend with hormones just now reaching their peak. Finding out that the parent who has been urging them to remain morally pure was himself willing to risk losing his home and family because he was unable to control his own hormones can seriously damage a teenager's ability to resist temptation. Writes Pittman, "The traumas of infidelity . . . are hardest on adolescents, who are sexually supercharged, and alternately delighted and terrified by sex. A parent's inability to maintain sexual control can be frightening, stimulating, and permissive."[4]

Adults need to acknowledge the seriousness of the emotional damage done to children and allow them time to heal. We dare not do them the injustice of assuming they possess the emotional and spiritual skills necessary to attend to their own injuries.

Beverly felt things would have been better for her children if Jim could have remained with the family. Our response to Beverly was, "But look at the mother God has given them in you." She has lived a life of dependence on God and of praise for

---

[4]Pittman, p. 263.

His faithfulness. Her children have been blessed with a parent whose life is a proven testimony of God's grace.

As difficult as the path ahead will be, mothers must realize that their children too have been blessed. She is their blessing, God's daily testimony of His grace in their lives. That doesn't mean she has to be perfect—just honest, loving, and patient. For one thing we do know is that healing requires big doses of all three.

7

And Jill Came Tumbling After

In the avalanche of people injured when a pastor falls, his wife is right there with him at the bottom of the heap. Her injuries and losses are legion. Gone are her sense of security, position of leadership and ministry, privacy, identity, and control over her own life. Her family, home, possessions, friends, money, confidence, spiritual foundation, and understanding of God's will—all are threatened.

A Christian life that she had considered to be well in order and designed by God is now turned totally upside down. No part of her life is untouched. It's a sudden, tragic death—the death of a relationship as she knew it.

Once bound by her husband's sin, she has now been set free by finding out the truth. To live in the light of this awful truth, however, is in many ways more terrifying than continuing to live in the darkness of the lie. At least the lie was familiar.

But reality is always preferable to ignorance. And truth is always preferable to lies. Even when it hurts.

Many people, especially Christians, have learned to deny the existence of personal hurt and apologize for tears. Rather than deal honestly with pain, they deny it. They spring up quickly after the fall, shake off those who offer help, and insist, "No, I'm okay. Everything's fine. Let's just get back to normal."

But there is no *normal*. What was normal is gone. Beverly could busy herself with the laundry but it didn't erase what she had seen in the kitchen.

Normal Must Be Redefined

For years, normal meant living by the same schedule—dinner at 6:30, shirts to the cleaners on Mondays, women's Bible study on Tuesday, church on Wednesdays, volunteer work on Thursday mornings. But suddenly there is no schedule. The old routine is meaningless, and the new one painful. Instead of busily doing for others, she is now having to take care of herself. And she cannot stop thinking—wondering how this could have happened, and worrying about what might lie ahead.

She is not ready to call friends or see family, knowing how easily one word or one look can start those tears flowing, tears she is trying so hard to quiet.

Her emotions are swinging on a pendulum set in motion by forces beyond her control. And no matter how spiritually strong she may be, no matter how much biblical truth she knows, she is still a fragile human being under extreme stress.

It is never easy to admit weakness, and when something goes wrong in our lives we immediately become vulnerable to outside censure and advice. For Christians that goes double. Love we can handle. Grief, anger, loneliness, and anxiety we cannot allow. A spouse's anger over her mate's adultery can become as much a target for condemnation as the adultery itself. Often those within the church will expect her to handle negative emotions without taking the time to work through them. Such an attitude can actually be damaging. If a spouse is denied the freedom to deal honestly and openly with her feelings and emotions, her recovery will slow down considerably. On the other hand, a church can facilitate the injured spouse's healing by ministering to her in these ways:

1. *Allow the spouse to express her feelings.* When it comes to expressing sadness, she probably needs a little encouragement. Even if she is not one to cry outwardly, she is experiencing a heavy sorrow within. Remind her that sorrow is honest; tears are a gift. We may not be comfortable, but as members of the body we can handle her tears. God weeps when we weep. He gathers our tears into bottles.[1] She needs a community of believers who realize that the sorrow she is experiencing is necessary.

In his book *The Complete Divorce Recovery Handbook*, John Splinter writes, "Facing and identifying feelings is critical to an individual's healing. . . . A person is far more in control when able to verbalize the actual feelings being experienced."

While it's acceptable for women to be sad or afraid, to cry, to withdraw out of helplessness, Splinter explains, they are "taught not to express anger or aggression."[2] He writes that "anger must be faced and managed. Unexpressed or unresolved anger is one of the primary, perhaps *the* primary,

---

[1]Psalm 56:8, King James Version.
[2]John P. Splinter, *The Complete Divorce Recovery Handbook* (Grand Rapids: Zondervan, 1992), p. 44.

source of clinical depression." While he warns that Christians often have difficulty resolving anger, since they "mistakenly believe their faith does not allow for its expression," he warns that eventually all suppressed anger is certain to erupt, "either internally or externally."[3]

Anger is the hardest emotion to acknowledge and confront. It's the most difficult to control and the one that most seriously threatens our self-image and our relationships to those around us. But when a person has been betrayed, anger is the most common and the most natural emotion.

In *Torn Asunder: Recovering from Extramarital Affairs*, Dave Carder cites some benefits of anger. He says that "anger shows we care, by the enormous amount of emotional passion we invest in it. . . . It's a positive, vital force that gives us energy, which can ward off depression. . . . Anger forces us to stop, to really hear what's being said and talk back. . . . Anger is honest—a welcome reality amidst the confusion of lies. . . . Anger pushes us to survive, to fight for answers and commitments."[4]

Feelings are nothing to be afraid of. Used properly, they will eventually aid in the healing.

2. *Don't place false blame on the spouse.* In most of our churches, adultery is failure with a capital F, and not just for the adulterer. If a mate goes outside of marriage for fulfillment, we point at the spouse for failing to meet his needs.

It's not easy for a wife to escape that finger. Even in current Christian texts we read that "people usually stay within the boundaries of marriage if their

---

[3]Splinter, p. 23.
[4]Dave Carder with Duncan Jaenicke, *Torn Asunder: Recovering from Extramarital Affairs* (Chicago: Moody, 1992), pp. 173–175.

primary [ego] needs are being adequately met,"[5] and that "many times the anguish of [an] affair is deepened because of an internal sense of failure on the part of the spouse . . . [who] knows that if she had done things differently she might not be in this position."[6]

The finger of guilt sometimes seems inescapable.

When Greg failed to be named president of his new business, Denise felt his deep disappointment. She sensed his emotional needs. She also realized they weren't talking the way they once had, daily discussing the important things as well as the trivial. But she had no reason to think the change in his behavior was due to anything other than his stressful career.

Beverly spoke of the time during Jim's absence when she realized how little she missed him. She was shocked by the awareness that her marriage lacked passion, that their love had become like a comfortable shoe. But lack of passion can have many causes other than adultery.

Another pastor's wife told of having been lied to for so long that she existed in a state of continual confusion, of craziness, where nothing made sense. But people lie to cover up things far less serious than adultery.

So then, once the adultery became known, all three women were surprised. They felt stupid. How could they not have seen the truth?

Every marriage has its flaws, composed of imperfect human beings. Christianity does not teach

---

[5]Henry A. Virkler, *Broken Promises: Healing and Preventing Affairs in Christian Marriages* (Dallas: Word, 1992), p. 57.
[6]Carder, p. 147.

that two needy, sinful, fragile human beings united by the miracle of marriage will immediately (if ever) become one strong and perfect entity, enjoying sex as the ultimate panacea, and having all needs and deficiencies and weak spots magically removed. Yet many Christians behave as if that were true, and when their needs are not met they go elsewhere to find what they believe is rightfully theirs: satisfaction, acceptance, fulfillment, or whatever seems to be lacking. And many of us within the body give credibility to this idea when we imply that one only ventures outside of marriage when certain needs go unmet.

To say that adultery occurred *because* needs went unmet leaves out far too many steps along the way. Adultery is but one of many ways to handle unmet needs, and it occurs when one partner takes matters into his or her own hands and disobeys God's moral law by seeking personal gratification outside the confines of marriage.

Every marriage has two partners, and when one of them deceives, lies, and jeopardizes the relationship by choosing infidelity and unfaithfulness, the partner who has remained faithful, chaste, and honest is not equally guilty for the affair.

In *Private Lies: Infidelity and the Betrayal of Intimacy*, Dr. Frank Pittman writes, "The dissatisfaction in a marriage may or may not be a joint effort, but the decisions about how to deal with an intolerable situation are clearly individual." To say existing problems *caused* the affair "turns responsibility for ending the affair to the betrayed spouse."[7] He goes on to say, "No one can *make* someone have an affair.

---

[7]Dr. Frank Pittman, *Private Lies: Infidelity and the Betrayal of Intimacy* (New York: Norton, 1989), p. 46.

An affair is never someone else's fault. What's more, affairs should not be taken personally. If your spouse makes the decision and then has an affair, don't assume you caused it. Don't let anybody talk you into believing that you made it happen."[8]

Sin happens because, for the moment, it seems pleasant and exciting, and because it offers instant comfort and temporary happiness. The joy of the moment obliterates both conscience and common sense. It negates for the time all fear of consequences; it ignores restraints. We see it, we want it, we choose it, we do it. And we are responsible before God for that choice.

3. *Help the spouse reestablish her own identity.* The pastor's wife has been Mrs. Somebody for a long time, and even if her marriage continues, her identity has been blurred. Yet long before she was married she had an identity of her own. Her task now is to find it, dust it off, and put it back in use. While a portion of who she is may be up for grabs, she still is the person God created her to be.

She is smart, capable, compassionate . . . vibrant, fun to be with . . . lovely, open, dependable, faithful . . . a good parent . . . appealing, talented, generous, kind . . . easygoing, funny, determined. Tell her so. Build her up. And help her find new ways to make use of her talents and strengths.

Applaud each of her victories, no matter how small they seem—whether checking the classifieds for job opportunities, calling for an interview, going out alone in public, or simply getting out of bed and facing the day.

4. *Help her learn to laugh again.* Even in the most

---

[8]Pittman, p. 284.

difficult circumstances we *need* to hear ourselves laugh, to see the irony, the absurdity, in all the tragedy around us. Laughter puts things in perspective. It shows we're not defeated. Nothing is more encouraging, more hopeful, than laughter.

5. *Offer practical as well as spiritual help.* She is still part of the body of Christ, and the body functions best when serving one another. If her husband has chosen to continue in sin, her daily physical needs will be as critical as her ongoing spiritual ones. She may need help with her car, home, or finances, and it is the responsibility of other Christians to offer help in such a way that she does not lose her dignity or self-esteem.

We all like being the one who is able to give, who has all the answers, and has everything under control. As a pastor's wife she has long been comfortable playing such a role, and it is a difficult one to relinquish. But God doesn't allow any of us the comfort of such a role indefinitely. We need Him, and we need one another. We all are destined to do time on the bottom of some heap. At any given moment there exists within the body those who need assistance and those who can provide it, and the players are constantly changing.

6. *Give her time to heal.* Love is patient, God is patient, but Christians tend to get in a hurry. We live in a world where patience means waiting, and waiting means failure. Weakness. Inefficiency. We consider our lives far too important to be placed on hold. But that is exactly where we need to be during times of stress, indecision, and confusion. We all need to be waiting on God.

Healing is a process; it comes little by little. Others may appear to have healed more quickly, but don't impose another's time frame on her. While they may look good on the outside, we really have no idea how well they have healed within.

Recovery will come in small, sometimes imperceivable, increments, but it will come. And it will come faster if surrounding the hurting spouse is a body of Christians committed to upholding her in prayer, and to building her up through encouragement and love.

8

How Could We Not Know?

"The signs were everywhere! How did we miss them?"

"How could we have been so blind?"

In nearly every case of pastoral failure, some signs of trouble in the pastor's life and in his church existed before his sin became public. Indicators were present, and sometimes even obvious, but most church members, leaders as well as laity, missed them, ignored them, or just couldn't believe that what they were seeing or sensing could really be true. And often they simply didn't know how to interpret the signals. So hints of trouble, which in hindsight were damning, were explained away, dismissed, or denied.

But later, after the swirling dust settles at the disaster site, people say, "You know, we had an idea something wasn't quite right."

"Looking back, I should have known."

We always think we should have known. We should have been able to intervene, to stop the offender. We should have been able to see that he was living a lie. That he was not the man we believed him to be. And perhaps, in some cases, we should have been able to see, to intervene, to take steps to confront the offender before the deadly effect of sin could poison others and infect the body of believers.

Perhaps in the future some churches, led by godly individuals, may be able to act sooner to confront sin, to call a leader to accountability, to offer discipline and restoration if Christians can learn to discern some of the signs of a troubled ministry.

How unfair (not to mention irresponsible!) it would be to suggest that there exists a distinct behavior pattern that every adulterous leader follows. There is none. Nor would it be fair (or responsible) to suggest that a leader is guilty of sexual misconduct because, in one isolated incident, his behavior was similar to that of a philanderer described in these pages.

But it is fair, and responsible, for Christians to agree that certain behavior is inappropriate, unseemly, and indicative of a troubled inner life.

Identifying Characteristics

After interviewing dozens of church members, listening to the stories of dozens of others, and studying multiple accounts of pastors' moral failures, we have been able to note that certain characteristics are common to churches where the leader was living a lie; where the pastor was guilty of sexual promiscuity.

1. *Several church members witnessed inappropriate behavior in their pastor.* In every church we studied where the pastor had indulged in sexual sin, he had been seen behaving inappropriately on many occasions.

One woman told of running into her pastor at

the local mall. While his wife bought cookies a few yards away, he stood and caressed the woman's arm, making eye contact that was extremely intimate and disconcerting for the woman.

"I was very uncomfortable," she said, "but then I thought, he wouldn't be coming on to me, he's the pastor."

Yes, he was the pastor. But yes, he was "coming on to her." Some months later he resigned amid allegations of ten or more affairs with women in his church.

In another church, an elderly woman told of seeing her pastor kissing a staff member's wife.

"It wasn't a peck on the cheek," she said. "It was a real kiss!" She was appalled, embarrassed, but thought she must be mistaken. Maybe it wasn't what it appeared to be.

A salesman who travels a lot saw his pastor in another town with a woman other than his wife. The man was uncertain about what he should do. He could have misread the situation, but he didn't really think so. Still he told himself there must be a reasonable explanation. There wasn't.

In one disconcerting instance, a teenage boy who was friends with the pastor's son came home after a visit in the parsonage. He told his parents about watching cable television and being embarrassed when a very explicit sexual scene came on the screen. The teenager blushed and fidgeted and finally left the room, but the pastor watched intently, never flinching. Later, the pastor's predilection for sexual fantasy and promiscuity made the newspapers. Only then did the teenager's mother voice the concerns she had felt over that incident.

"That really bothered my husband and me," she

said, "but what do you do?"

If you're like most folks in a church family, you feel uncomfortable. You wonder. You think that a man who presents himself as a leader of God's people should have different preferences in entertainment; he should exercise better judgment; and at the very least he should be more cautious around weaker brothers—especially teenage boys!

People recognized something wasn't quite right. But like most folks, they did nothing. Except feel confused and disoriented.

Contradictory behavior does that to us. And Christians who have to deal with it begin to doubt their own veracity. They begin to think maybe they are a little crazy, a little too reactionary. Surely the pastor wouldn't do anything as gross as . . . or would he?

In *Private Lies: Infidelity and the Betrayal of Intimacy,* Dr. Frank Pittman, a psychiatrist and family therapist, writes about an environment where a spouse is guilty of infidelity: "People who are lied to become dependent, anxious, delicate, and over-reactive." In that same discussion he says that if a partner is lied to long enough, he or she is bound to "seem rather crazy."[1]

This symptom showed up many times in our study of the subject of pastoral infidelity. The congregation of a lying, cheating pastor feels disoriented, confused. They sense something isn't right, but they don't know exactly what is wrong. Some members admit to feeling a little crazy themselves.

Uncertain that there is a problem, uncertain of their instincts and intuition—they dare not even

---

[1] Dr. Frank Pittman, *Private Lies: Infidelity and the Betrayal of Intimacy* (New York: Norton, 1989), p. 66.

think that their pastor is capable of such evil, much less speak of it. But they are troubled, fragile, anxious. Entire congregations, if they are lied to long enough, grow fearful, over-reactive, and confused.

In each of the cases we studied, as well as the ones we experienced personally, we found people who didn't want to believe that their pastors could be so dishonest, so deceitful, so wicked. And yet, in each case, members recalled incidents that were disconcerting—things that were troubling—long before the pastor's sin was revealed.

2. *Members, staff, and laity felt they were being manipulated by the pastor.* Although some pastors are manipulative and coercive without being adulterers (see *The Subtle Power of Spiritual Abuse* by Dave Johnson and Jeff VanVonderen), in every case we encountered where the pastor was involved in sexual sin, he was known for coercing others into supporting activities and endeavors they did not favor. Using guilt mixed with praise and flattery, he controlled many members of his congregation. And that control enabled him to escape accountability.

An elder in a conservative midwestern Bible church told about feeling confused and concerned when the pastor asked for $15,000 to soundproof his office. Funds were tight, so the request was denied, but a short time later, when the church embarked on a building program, a $30,000 soundproof package for the pastor's office was approved. "Why does he need lead lining in his walls?" the elder wanted to know. The pastor explained, "I deal with intimate, eternal issues in counseling, and I need to be sure that confidences will not be violated."

Later, it became obvious why the pastor needed

to ensure his privacy. He was seducing women in his windowless office and arranging future liaisons behind his lead-lined walls.

It is common for an errant pastor to coerce and spiritually manipulate his staff, elders, deacons, and parishioners to achieve his own ends. Often, his ends is the protection of his secret, and the lengths to which he must go to achieve that are extreme. Like lead-lined walls in a windowless office.

3. *Strong members of the congregation were denigrated by the pastor.* These members are the ones likely to insist on accountability. They are the ones who will question inappropriate behavior, and so the pastor must take great pains to keep them out of places of authority. These men and women are too strong for him to control—they are his worst enemies.

In committee meetings, these individuals are not afraid to question the pastor's plans, his philosophy of ministry, his goals for the church, and his personal lifestyle. The pastor knows these leaders are spiritually minded and this causes him great concern. He must find ways to shield himself from their discernment. He must find ways to separate them from the decision-making boards within the body. He must weaken their influence and make sure that less mature, less discerning members sit in places of authority.

Several pastors who were hiding promiscuity attempted to drive away strong, mature believers. This was not an easy thing to do, however, because in most cases these lay leaders had long-standing ties to the congregation and were not willing to quietly walk away from family-like bonds.

If all else fails, the adulterous pastor may resort to direct attack. Using spiritual jargon and theological rhetoric to silence those who challenge him, he will attempt to make them out as enemies of progress and ministry.

In one church in suburban Chicago, a philandering pastor felt especially threatened by one elder. The congregation loved and respected this older man, one of the founders of the church and one who had poured the foundation and laid the bricks for the building in which they worshiped. The elder had long been considered a good Bible teacher in the adult Sunday school department when the pastor began a nasty campaign to discredit him.

"He's not a theologian," the pastor said of the elder. "He is completely missing the point of that passage," he whispered to members as they exited their class on Sunday mornings, adding under his breath, "I really don't think he should be teaching a Sunday school class."

Little by little, the pastor undermined the elder, destroying his credibility, questioning his doctrine, and openly ridiculing his teaching skills. In board meetings, he called the man critical and unloving and branded him a hindrance to the ministry because he insisted on accountability and expected the pastor to explain rumors concerning inappropriate behavior.

In time, the pastor's sexual habits became known and the elder was vindicated, but not before the church had traveled down a long road into chaos. And not before the elder's heart was broken.

4. *There was dissension in the church.* In every case of pastoral promiscuity we studied, the congrega-

tion was torn with divisions. Some were worse than others, but all had a serious, if not loudly addressed, problem of disunity.

One of the most tragic examples of disunity occurred in the suburban church mentioned above where the elder confronted the pastor with rumors about promiscuity. In a brilliant defensive move, the pastor denied everything and turned to the elder's brother, also on the elder board, for support. Driving a wedge into a family that had worshiped together all their lives, the pastor convinced one brother to turn against the other. Within the congregation of about 350, several factions lined up against each other. Life-long friends fought each other, devoured each other, and forgot about the love and commitment to worship and service that had brought them together in the first place.

In Andrea's church, the pastor kept his congregation divided and created friction among members and between husbands and wives by repeating private conversations. Perhaps it was a deliberate ploy to keep the congregation in small, manageable chunks, in case he should need to rally support in a hurry. Or it may have been a result of his inability to discern the Holy Spirit's leading in matters of unity—the consequence of living in habitual sin. Either way, the body suffered with schisms and factions, often very painful ones that threatened to sever even family ties.

5. *Several women within the congregation knew inappropriate intimate details about the pastor.* In a large majority of the cases we examined, older women in the church had heard suggestive information from younger women in the church—information that hinted at a more intimate relationship than any pas-

tor and parishioner should have. One woman learned that the pastor was making late night phone calls to a younger woman in the church and disclosing very personal information about his marriage. In casual conversation, the younger woman mentioned some of these intimate details.

In another case, a Sunday school teacher heard one of her young students talk about the pastor in a very personal, intimate way. "I was troubled by that," the teacher said later, "but I didn't know what to do."

Another woman told of visiting a young, recently divorced mother. "This young woman opened a cupboard and showed me she had stocked up on a particular food item because it was Pete's [the pastor's] favorite." Everything the younger woman said and did suggested that her pastor spent a lot of time in her home. The older woman knew this was not a good situation, but she cast off her suspicions as nasty thoughts and decided that to do anything about it would be meddling. Later it became known that the pastor was sexually involved with the woman.

6. *The preaching was weak.* When a pastor is living a lie, his preaching eventually is affected. When inquiring about the preaching of errant pastors, we learned that congregants were most often troubled by one of three things: (1) Sermons were abusive and harsh. Pastors often "beat the sheep," scolding them instead of leading them, blaming them for whatever ills existed within the congregation, and using guilt-producing rhetoric to shame them into submission; (2) Sermons were based on New Age ideas, positive mental attitude concepts, half-truths, or blatant false doctrine rather than on

sound biblical truth; (3) Previously meaty messages of truth became weak and watered down. Biblical teaching was diluted until the message was barely recognizable as authoritative.

In only one church did a former member say that the pastor's sermons remained good even up to the final Sunday he preached. "He was always prepared," the member said. "His doctrine was sound, and his points were strong."

"Yes," agreed another member, "but toward the end it was like he was delivering a recipe for a chocolate cake."

As the power of this man's life diminished, the power of his preaching vanished. He knew the words, but they no longer rang with passion. Unable or unwilling to relate the truth to his own life, he could no longer make it meaningful or relevant to others.

How could it be any other way? The things of God are spiritually discerned, and if the messenger is living a life that has quenched the Spirit, his sermons will reflect his heart. "Out of the abundance of the heart the mouth speaketh," Jesus said (Matthew 12:34, KJV).

It may be possible to fool some of the people some of the time, as the saying goes, but it is not possible to fool all the people all the time. Spiritually discerning members will notice that something is awry. They may not know exactly what it is, but they will sense that something is not right.

Ironically, some promiscuous pastors have been known to deliver stinging sermons complete with terrifying indictments against sexual sin, as did one nationally known televangelist just days before the account of his promiscuous behavior made headline news. But in most of the cases we studied, pastors pursuing a sinful lifestyle cut a large path around issues of morality and sexual conduct, preferring to focus on any one of the myriad of topics suitable for a Sunday morning sermon.

The sad reality is this: In a large majority of the churches we observed, the adulterous pastor's lifestyle did affect his preaching, and the sheep that followed him, expecting to be fed, were instead either beaten, poisoned, or starved.

Don't Assume There Is Sexual Sin

It is terrifying to think that someone might misunderstand and misuse the information in this chapter. So, for the sake of caution, let us say again that disunity, disgruntled elders, or a less-than-inspiring sermon now and then are not absolute indicators that the pastor is involved in sin.

No church has ever been problem free. Unity will always be a challenge. Preaching will please some and displease others. Leaders, lay and otherwise, will engage in power struggles on occasions. But ongoing sexual sin within a church presents uniquely serious problems. And signs will abound, whether subtle or blatant. Because no sin exists in isolation.

Responding to the Signs

So what do Christians do when they observe signs of a troubled ministry? What do they do when confronted with mounting evidence that something is awry in their pastor's life? When suspicions cannot be ignored? How long do they wait? How many troubling situations will they try to explain away or forget?

Perhaps a better question is this: "Why do we try so hard to pretend nothing is wrong?"

Two reasons come to mind. First, we don't want to believe our leader is guilty of misconduct. We want to believe there are reasonable explanations for the behavior we find upsetting and confusing. We want to believe the best. After all, we have trusted him with our spiritual needs. We don't like the idea that we might have been deceived and betrayed.

Second, we don't like to contemplate the risks that accompany the confrontation of sin. In plain language, we're scared. It's a terrifying experience to stand toe-to-toe against sin. Maybe it shouldn't be—we're covered by the blood of Christ and we're dressed in spiritual armor (if we've taken time to put it on). But fear is a reasonable emotion to have before entering a war zone.

And wherever sin is present, war is raging. Damage and injuries are likely. Fear is not only reasonable, it is useful. Fear is useful if it drives us to our knees and makes us cry out to God for power and courage to deal with the problems in our church. It is useful if it awakens in us a new sense of urgency to protect the body of Christ. It is useful if it makes us cautious and causes us to seek wisdom before voicing any concerns we have about our spiritual leaders. And it is useful if it makes us take a fresh look at how we perceive ourselves in relationship to our churches and to the men and women who lead them.

9

The Question of Confrontation

Confrontation can be costly.

The elder who called for his pastor to explain questionable behavior found himself ostracized, belittled, and accused of being unloving.

The salesman who tried to get someone to listen to his concerns about the pastor was ridiculed and labeled a troublemaker.

When several women reported that their pastor was making abusive sexual advances toward them they were called emotional, hormonal, immature. An elder in their denomination even called them unstable.

Accounts of individual believers trying to confront sin in a leader are often accompanied by stories of their own mistreatment. Actually, it is unrealistic to expect anything else. After all, if the pastor is living a sin-filled life, he is not likely to respond to the charges by saying, "Thanks, I was hoping someone would notice."

In most of the cases we studied, unpleasantness followed confrontation. Members willing to come forward and address sin in their leader quickly realized that the experience was not going to be fun. For many, it meant giving up a comfortable place in the pew. It meant losing friends as battle lines were drawn. It meant sadness, strife, and often a deep sense of loss as they came to terms with the inevitable changes that took place in their church and even in their most cherished relationships.

What Makes It Worth the Cost?

There is only one answer: obedience. Obedience is always worth the cost. And yes, it is a matter of obedience.

As the body of Christ, we are responsible for maintaining its purity as well as for living out the character of God before the world.

We are responsible for one another. Jesus himself said so (Matthew 5 and 18) and so did the apostle Paul (Galatians 1:6). And every mention of the church as a body with its interconnected and interdependent parts further illustrates this principle.

We are called to minister to one another. And the act of confronting sin in our leaders—or insisting that signs of trouble in our leaders' lives be addressed—is part of our ministry to one another. It is not only the pastor who is responsible to speak out against sin. As members, we too must be alert to its dangers.

We can't escape the meaning here: My pastor is my responsibility as much as I am his. But in many congregations little is understood about the idea of ministering to our pastors as equal members of the body. We expect them to minister to us; we expect our local congregations to become involved in ministries to the poor and downtrodden; we establish mission boards to ensure ministry to the lost, both at home and abroad. But we have little or no concept of the congregation ministering to its pastor.

For many churchgoers, ministering to their pastor means putting an extra twenty dollars in the offering plate or taking him shopping for a new suit when the old one starts to show signs of wear. But a spiritual leader's needs cannot be met by covering him in a new Sunday suit. Pastors, as well as the members they serve, need people in their lives who will speak the truth to them; people who are spiritually discerning and willing to confront them when something doesn't seem right.

Giving and Taking Correction in a Responsible Manner

A middle-aged pastor in a small church in the Northwest was confronted one day by a younger member who was very concerned because a recent sermon seemed to reflect a less than godly attitude toward finances.

"He thought I was out of line," the pastor said. "He made his case very kindly, and with a humble but firm manner. I had to listen to him and reexamine what I had said and how I had said it. We spent about two hours together talking about attitudes and scripture.

"I know it took a lot of courage for him to come to me and I really admire him for it. I defended some of my statements, and he agreed he may have misunderstood some things, but he hadn't misunderstood my attitude, and he thought it needed a good checking. The idea of being confronted wasn't really enjoyable at first, but I know I needed that young man to come and talk to me. I'd had a chance to get to know his heart and I know he came to me out of love."

How wonderful it would be if every occasion of confrontation could be as productive and as loving. Of course, when the problem is more serious, more potentially explosive, the circumstances are much more difficult. Much more frightening.

How hard it is to imagine stepping into our pastor's office and telling him we have seen him behave in an inappropriate way with a woman other than his wife! Or that we have heard numerous accounts that suggest he is practicing promiscuity. This is the man who stands in the pulpit week after week and delivers God's Word to us. He is our spiritual leader. It is difficult to contemplate a confrontation with him. It is awkward, frightening.

For centuries, pastors/priests have been present and in control at the most intimate, meaningful moments of our lives. We have entrusted them with the power to marry us and to bury us. We have disclosed to them our deepest secrets. Only God knows many of the things we have shared with our spiritual leaders. No wonder we are frightened. No wonder we delay as long as possible. No wonder we pretend the signs around us are simply tricks of our imagination. We just cannot summon the courage to confront the one we perceive as a powerful individual.

But is this a correct perception of the church? That one individual would be "in charge," elevated above the rest? That leaders in the Christian church should be viewed as superior to the ordinary churchgoer? That members should be intimidated by their pastors?

Scripture contradicts that view by telling all

Christians to take responsibility for one another. We are all sheep, fed by the same Shepherd, led along the same paths of righteousness. One is not greater than another. Each of us has the right and the responsibility to identify sin wherever it is found. If we observe signs of habitual sin in the life of a fellow-believer, we are charged to minister to him, regardless of his vocation. And the most loving act we can take toward him is confrontation.

Our spiritual leaders are a part of the body of Christ, and their lives and welfare are our concern, just as ours are his. Jesus has charged us with confrontation as well as with reconciliation.

How Do We Go About It?

What do we say? To whom do we say it first?

These are essential questions, because ministries can be cut down, lives and marriages destroyed by a wrong word or a misplaced comment. And we can't find answers by relying on our instincts. We have to rely on the Scriptures.

Jesus' first recorded sermon—Matthew 5—addresses the issues of interpersonal relationships, confrontation, and restoration. And how like Christ to preface a plan of action with a careful presentation of right attitudes. The first sermon out of Jesus' mouth gives us what we know as the Beatitudes:

Blessed are the poor in spirit . . .
Blessed are those who mourn . . .
Blessed are the meek . . .
Blessed are those who hunger and thirst for righteousness . . .
Blessed are the merciful . . .
Blessed are the pure in heart . . .

Blessed are the peacemakers . . .
Blessed are those who are persecuted because of
   righteousness . . .
Blessed are you when people insult you, perse-
   cute you and falsely say all kinds of evil
   against you because of me . . .

Seated on a mountain, with His disciples at His feet and a vast colorful sea of humanity spilling out in the background, Jesus delivered Scripture's most compelling sermon. And while the beauty and power of His words were still ringing across the hillside, He went on to give practical teaching on how to address sin in a brother or sister.

We can't talk about confrontation and sin in another's life until we have first grasped the meaning of the Beatitudes and applied them to our own lives. We have to ask ourselves:

1. Do I understand the concept of spiritual poverty? That I have no spiritual wealth of my own to boast of? That I, along with all of humanity, am empty until Christ fills me?

2. Am I capable of feeling grief over sin? Do I mourn? Do I comprehend the horror, the magnitude of sin?

3. Does gentleness characterize me? Am I capable of dealing with a brother or sister without complicating the person's injuries or inflicting further harm?

4. Do I crave righteousness? Or am I secretly pleased by the thought of seeing someone brought down in shame?

5. Am I familiar enough with mercy to be able to offer it to others? Or am I excited about the prospect of vengeance?

6. Am I known as a peacemaker? Or am I known

as one who spreads discord? What motives characterize me among the body of Christ?

7. Am I willing to accept whatever personal hurt I will encounter on the route to righteousness? Am I quick to shrink from the possibility of pain?

8. Does the thought of being misunderstood or rejected deter me from pursuing what I know is right?

We cannot consider confrontation until these questions have been answered adequately, truthfully. Because unless the spiritual traits found in Jesus' words characterize us, we are not prepared to carry out the task of confronting and reconciling.

Self-Examination

The language of Matthew 5:23–24 calls for self-examination—an important step for all of us, but especially for one who is considering addressing the sin of another. Is there anyone in your congregation who has reason to feel offended by something you've done? Is there a misunderstanding that needs to be cleared up in your life? Do it now, Jesus says. Don't rationalize or justify bad behavior or conduct in your own life. Confess it. Reconcile with that one in your congregation to whom you owe an apology. Make it right.

It makes sense, doesn't it? If we are going to take responsibility for the health of the body of Christ, we must begin with ourselves. The commitment to purity within the church must begin within every individual believer.

Jesus again addresses the issue of reconciliation and confrontation (Matthew 18), and again He prefaces His words with the teaching of humility. "Except you be like a little child. . . ." Children are dependent and vulnerable, and for an adult to take on these characteristics requires humility. He issues a stern warning to any who would harm His precious children, and then He reminds us of our immeasurable value to God.

With those words echoing in the disciples' ears, Jesus then talked to them about how to deal with a brother who was practicing sin. We must remember humility; we must not forget our own vulnerability. Knowing this, we tread carefully, not wanting to do or say anything that would hinder the repentance of the one who is being disobedient.

Step One

Cautiously, we step onto the threshold of confrontation. Alone, the first time. One to one, according to Jesus. "Go and reprove him in private," Jesus said. If he listens, you've won him.

Paul repeats Jesus' instructions in Titus 1, and adds, if the one we're confronting is an elder, don't rebuke him sharply. Appeal to him as a father. With respect, with humility, as you would a family member. He may be an elder by position—your pastor or a visible leader in another capacity within the body; or he may be simply an elder by age. Paul's meaning here is clear, however. Let your manner and your words show the respect due his age or position.

In some situations, however, a sharp rebuke will be necessary. In Titus 1:13, Paul adds the adverb "severely." Reprove severely—with the intent to produce conviction.

Step Two

Sometimes step one isn't enough.

"But if he doesn't listen to you, take one or two more with you, so that by the mouth of two or three witnesses every fact may be confirmed," Jesus instructed.

The "witnesses" aren't eye witnesses to the pastor/leader's misconduct. In this passage, based on Mosaic law, they are witnesses to the procedure and the outcome of the confrontation. However, in 1 Timothy 5:17, Paul adds this to Jesus' words: "Do not receive an accusation against an elder except on the basis of two or three witnesses." This passage suggests that in the case of accusations against an elder or leader, the witnesses should be able to supply evidence of wrongdoing.

In *A Guide to Church Discipline*, J. Carl Laney explains that this New Testament passage offers a safeguard for the pastor, protecting him from false charges that might have been fabricated by a disgruntled member. Dr. Laney writes:

"In addition to strengthening the rebuke, the context seems to suggest that Paul is concerned that the elder not be subjected to slander or personal attack. The requirement of testimony from witnesses would serve as a precautionary measure against unjust and unverified accusations."[1]

Sometimes the process of confrontation ends with this step. With brokenness, repentance, and the implementation of a plan for discipline and restoration. Sometimes it ends with nothing but angry recriminations. Sometimes nothing is resolved.

---

[1] J. Carl Laney, *A Guide to Church Discipline* (Minneapolis: Bethany House Publishers, 1985), p. 62.

Step Three

"If he refuses to listen to them [the two or three], tell it to the church."

Jesus doesn't spell out exactly how to do this, nor do Paul's letters to the churches. Some congregations may decide it's best to gather in small groups for disclosure. Others may choose to make the matter known all at one time to the entire congregation. Scripture leaves it to individual churches to make that call, under the direction of the Holy Spirit.

And now, here is one more chance for repentance.

By informing the whole church, several safeguards are put into place. First, the decisions made concerning the errant pastor will not be left to a single person. The whole body is a part of the process. Second, by involving the entire congregation, church discipline can be implemented according to Paul's teaching in the New Testament epistles. (*A Guide to Church Discipline* offers an excellent treatise on the subject.) Third, the burden of handling the crisis is not relegated to one or two who could be labeled "the bad guys." It allows the entire body to participate in "tough love." And fourth, by handling the crisis openly there is less secrecy, which so often breeds lies, rumors, and fear.

Step Four

But what if the offender still refuses to repent after the offense is made known to the whole church? The church has done its part, decently and in order, according to scriptural teachings, though not without great emotional strain. But the one who has caused it all remains stubborn and unrepentant. What happens next?

Jesus tells us to treat him as if he were an unbeliever. A tax collector. A Gentile.

Does that mean we are to cut him loose, heave him out, and never associate with him again?

Remember Jesus' opening words in Matthew 5 and His teachings in Matthew 18. We are to be like children: trusting and vulnerable.

Based on Jesus' example, and the context of His teaching, there is no room for believers implementing discipline to become haughty, abusive, or unloving. Instead, their task is to win back the errant one. There is little chance of this happening if he is treated rudely and unkindly.

The urgent task of the church is to demonstrate the character of God toward the lost. The one who has been removed from our midst fits that category. He is in need of being found. He is in need of prayer. He is in need of the truth. The truth is that sin separates; sin injures; sin kills. By considering the unrepentant brother as an unbeliever, we are able to demonstrate not only hatred for sin but also deep concern for the health and safety of the whole body.

The church members who have had to participate in his discipline will be challenged, perhaps on a daily basis, to examine their attitudes. Are they sorrowful? Or secretly glad he's getting his comeuppance? Are they hurting for him and his family, as well as for their church? Have they genuine concern for the health and safety of the whole body?

Dr. Laney's careful study of all the passages that address church discipline leaves us no room to argue with the teaching that in some instances Christians within a local church *will have to withdraw the hand of fellowship from an unrepentant member* who refuses to stop living in habitual sin. This includes unrepentant leaders as well.

It is done as a last resort. It is done for the sake of the whole body. It is done not only to discipline the sinful one, but also to provide safety for all the others. The purity of the body of Christ is at stake.

It is done not with glee nor vengeance, but with humility and grief. While we may be able to forbid this one from joining in fellowship with us, we cannot forbid his entry into heaven. We can avoid associating ourselves with his wicked lifestyle, but it is not in our power to void his salvation. We cannot welcome him into our church while he is blatantly defying God, but we can pray for him and behave kindly toward him when we encounter him on the street, in the store, or at a neighborhood soccer game. If he is married, we can reach out to his wife and children and try to relieve their anguish.

The Loving Action of the Body of Christ

Long before a congregation makes that final, painful break with an unrepentant leader, one lone member has wrestled with uncertainty, indecision, and fear. It is most often a private, agonized wrestling as he or she tries to discern the meaning of a witnessed impropriety, a rumor, a report of misconduct, or the mounting signs of a ministry gone awry.

Before going to the pastor/leader with concerns about perceived impropriety, many members have sought the counsel of older, trusted believers. Overwhelmed and uncertain, they just didn't know what else to do. Throughout Proverbs, Solomon tells us to seek counsel, that there is wisdom in asking for help. For individuals suddenly forced to carry the weight of knowledge too heavy for them, the support and wisdom of a spiritual mentor made the difference between total chaos and the orderly handling of a sensitive, potentially devastating matter.

Those we interviewed who had prayerfully and humbly confronted sin in a leader had done so with full knowledge of the risks. They recognized there would be consequences. But they preferred the consequences of action to those of inaction. As sheep of the same flock, they took responsibility for one another. They took responsibility for the life and conduct of a leader they loved. They risked censure, misunderstanding, and rejection in order to rebuke sin.

It wasn't easy. But it was loving.

Loving action. That is what the body of Christ is called to perform. It is loving because it offers the offender the opportunity to repent; loving because it refuses to tolerate sin or enable the sinner to continue in his waywardness; and loving because such actions prevent further injury to the local congregation.

As responsible members of the body of Christ, we have no choice but to respond to the presence of sin within the church. It is never easy and it is never fun (beware of anyone who seems to enjoy it). And for some it will be excruciating. The risk is great—pain and suffering are inevitable. But the alternative, allowing sin to run rampant within the body, is ultimately devastating.

We must each see ourselves as vital members of

the body, each entrusted with the care of the whole. As God assigns us responsibility, He also provides power and discernment. And He assures us that no matter what kind of danger assaults our church, "the very gates of hell shall not prevail against it."

Recognizing and confronting sin in ourselves and in our leaders is as much a part of the ministry of the body as baptizing, preaching, and teaching. It is the means by which the body remains pure and powerful, prepared to undertake the tasks Christ has assigned to it. It is the means by which purity can be defined in a world that has no other frame of reference.

We must not be afraid to minister to one another. Even if the sheep in need is the one in the lead.

10

Working Through
the Aftermath

A Growing Problem

A parking lot where a church used to stand.

A tiny cluster of believers huddled together for comfort in a small room.

Twentieth-century Christians in America are not accustomed to such images of themselves and their places of worship. We are proud of our buildings and our building programs. We like numbers and high-attendance Sundays and a long list of outreach ministries. But in spite of our enjoyment of what we define as success, our countryside is littered with the debris of once-thriving, now-fallen, churches. In nearly every U.S. city there are sites where churches used to stand, where congregations once numbering in the hundreds, some in the thousands, have shriveled to little more than a handful.

You talk with a Christian in Arizona and find out that his pastor had an affair with a woman in the congregation. You discover that your friend's sister in Colorado attended a church with the same problem. You visit with an old school friend in Missouri and learn that the church down the street folded after the minister ran away with his secretary. You can mention the topic almost anywhere and hear about adulterous pastors up and down the eastern seaboard, across the plains, and on to the Pacific coast. You can't discuss the subject of infidelity for very long before you learn that almost everyone you speak to has a story about a church, a pastor, and a community that was deeply hurt by the sin.

Often you'll hear comments like this: "Our church was never the same after that," "A lot of our people just never got over it," and sometimes, oftentimes, "I just never could go to church after that."

We may be able to count the number of churches that are damaged by a leader's sexual sin—in some cities you can keep a weekly tally from local newspapers—but we can't begin to calculate the number of individuals harmed when these leaders fell.

In one New Mexico diocese alone, more than three hundred thousand parishioners are coping with the agony and fear surrounding allegations of sexual misconduct within the priesthood.[1] Add to that figure another ten thousand—the members of a church you'll read about in this chapter; and to that, add another one thousand from Andrea's church. The numbers swell daily. And who can say how many more are struggling with spiritual confusion due to the failure of men and women who present themselves as authorities on matters of the soul?

When victims are lying at the bottom of the heap, crushed by the weight of another's sin, can

---

[1]*Dallas Morning News*, April 11, 1993, 37A.

they be helped back to their feet, restored to a faithful stance?

The answer to this question is yes. Absolutely, categorically yes!

Those crushed by the sin of their leaders can be restored. Their faith can be infused with new confidence and assurance. And their lives can grow strong and be useful to God and His kingdom.

But for most hurting, disillusioned Christians, even the mature ones, healing doesn't happen overnight. Restored faith and vision are not accomplished easily nor quickly. Multiple applications of wisdom and grace and patience seem to be the best treatment for sorrowing, sickened souls.

When Your Pastor Makes the Front Page

The members of First Church awoke one fine spring day to find the face of their pastor on the front page of the newspaper. "Pastor resigns amid allegations of sexual misconduct," the headlines read.

Misery, like a heavy blanket, settled over the church. Questions and rumors swirled. Ten thousand men, women, and children found themselves being dragged into the sordid story of their pastor's promiscuity. As members of a single body, they shared his humiliation. They could not escape his embarrassment, nor their own sense of betrayal.

The remaining staff, scrambling to maintain a schedule of services, outreach ministries, and a budget that would pay the mortgage on the multi-million-dollar buildings, shifted the load among themselves and the church elders. They called an interim pastor to fill the pulpit and tried to forge a plan that would enable them to keep the church doors open.

On the following Sunday, the congregation quietly entered the worship center, their eyes glazed and their faces looking shell-shocked. Subdued, and somewhat smaller in number than in previous weeks, the crowd sat in numbed silence as an associate pastor, battling his own fragile emotions, swallowed, and greeted them in a somber, halting voice.

"We will continue to go forward," he said. "This church is larger than one man, and we will continue with the ministries that we have begun."

His manner humble, his countenance sad, the associate minister offered the congregation these assurances: Nothing will change. Stay with us. Pray with us. And don't worry; we can weather this storm.

The youth pastor delivered the sermon that day, a sermon on faith. After a final prayer and the choral response, the congregation was dismissed.

Anger Wants to Place Blame

But beyond the sanctuary, in classrooms throughout the educational wing, a very different scene was playing. Inside those rooms, behind closed doors, the adult Sunday school classes met, and there dull eyes sparked as if struck by flint. Sharp words cut the somber silence, and anger rather than despair was the dominant emotion.

In these small groups, where men and women had come together for study and prayer and fellowship, where rapport and trust had been established, there were no hushed voices. Strident sounds of anger echoed in some rooms. Occasional chuckles could even be heard—sardonic, self-effacing chuckles—no real humor, no true mirth. Just honest-to-goodness responses to grief and disappointment.

In one classroom where a handful of adults battled their emotions, one man asked, "Why didn't we see it coming? How did he live a lie for so long and no one knew?"

Another said, "I'm not surprised. His sermons had become so watered-down. There was no depth—sometimes I wondered if he'd been reading the same Bible I read. I was really concerned about his preaching."

A woman added, "I'm enraged! How could this have happened?"

Some cried softly.

Angry comments, heartbroken expressions, quiet tears, and the ever-present question: How could we have been fooled? Few offered any answers except to say the pastor's inner life was somehow skewed; that he had fooled himself as well as everyone else; that God would deal with him; that God was still God.

Week after week, in various small groups, church members expressed their anger, their grief, their sense of humiliation.

"That man performed my daughter's wedding ceremony!"

"I went to him for marriage counseling a few times," someone said.

"We trusted him to guide us, and look where he guided us—right onto the front pages of the newspaper."

Making Way for Healing

Years have passed since the name of First Church was smeared in the news, and the church has recovered its strength. Occasionally someone will ask, "Isn't that the church whose pastor resigned because of a sex scandal?" But most folks know First Church as a vital place where the gospel is preached without apology; where ministry extends beyond its manicured suburban exterior and into the city. Some folks think of First Church as the church that survived; the church that, in spite of the leader's failure, remained faithful.

More vibrant, more effective than anyone ever imagined it could be after its tragic loss of leadership, First Church tells us something about how a congregation is healed. Healing wasn't administered from the pulpit on Sunday mornings, or even on Sunday nights. It happened in small groups where the members of the body ministered to one another with sympathy, understanding, and openness. The choir members, close-knit after years of ministering and worshiping together, supported one another and allowed true feelings to be expressed in an atmosphere of love and acceptance. On Wednesday prayer services, when the congregation gathered for dinner, members sat together in small groups and talked about their feelings, God's faithfulness, and their determination to stay together as a body. Sometimes they cried, sometimes they hugged each other, but always they appeared to be supporting each other and allowing one another to grieve. The adult Sunday school classes were especially important during the church's time of deep disappointment and sadness.

While there are those who say that the Sunday school is out-dated and dying, these small groups, united in Bible study and bonded by common interests, maintained a level of spiritual continuity for many adults who may otherwise have opted to flee the scene of tragedy.

For many, the idea of running away was tempting. One adult teacher who had taught the same class for five years admitted that it would have been easy to leave and find another church, one without the smear of scandal. But the love and concern he felt for those in his class made him stay and be a part of his church's healing. Another Sunday school teacher said, "I felt like I was the pastor to my adult class. It was a small, intimate group of young couples, and suddenly they were looking to me for the kind of example and leadership the pastor had given them. I had an even stronger sense of the need to minister to them and to encourage them in their faith."

People at First Church responded to the tragedy much like one would respond to death. They passed through all the various stages of grief, moving from disbelief to horror and shock; then to deep sadness, and finally to acceptance. In most groups, someone wanted to know exactly what the pastor did. Did he have an affair? Was it a woman in the congregation? Who was she? Was there more than one? While the church leaders did not openly address those questions, the small groups asked them anyway and were not censored by each other for doing so. With occasional exceptions, the honest expression of emotions was accepted.

Every feeling, from rage to deep sadness, erupted. And finally, after a while, for most of the members of First Church, a kind of acceptance set-tled in. Acceptance of the horror and loss; accept-ance that human leaders will fail.

The Value of Small Groups

At First Church, little was said from the platform about the pastor's demise, just a few brief state-ments made the Sunday morning after the news story appeared.

An associate pastor explained the reasons:

"To offer any kind of open response to the sit-uation during a Sunday morning worship service, with more than three thousand people present, would have been an opportunity for pure chaos. How could we deal with so many people without inviting an out-of-control situation? But in the class-rooms, in the smaller groups, people could express their feelings and classes could pray together and encourage each other. I really think that was the key to our being able to survive this."

Like intensive care units, the small groups pro-vided an environment of intimate concern where members could recover and regain their strength. They learned together, through practical experi-ence, that God is truly preeminent; that His church will stand; that even the gates of hell cannot prevail against it. First Church's recovery was aided, per-haps, by the fact that the adulterous pastor left the church within hours after his admission of guilt. His family went with him, along with a small frag-ment of the congregation. The members left behind were not required to deal with his restoration or discipline. They were left to grieve and to find healing. And finally, to get back to the ministry of presenting Christ to a dying world.

An Announcement to Fell the Most Faithful

Ted Morris's church coped with its grief differently. Direct, head on, like a Mack truck crashing full speed into the side of mountain. Ted, the senior pastor, addressed his Sunday morning congregation of more than three thousand with a report that three of his fellow-ministers had admitted to sexual sin. Delivering the information with carefully chosen words, Ted talked plainly and without euphemism. In a sort of "play by play," he explained how he had learned of the activities, what his first response had been, what his first actions had been, and what he believed they, as a church body, should do next.

At times during his report (for it was more of a report than a sermon), Ted said, "I feel exhausted. I need God's energy." Then, leading the congregation in prayer, he asked, "Let grace flow."

No one listening to Ted could doubt that his heart was broken. His voice cracked occasionally, but he continued on in his direct approach toward the disaster site. Without hedging, he told of the behavior of those who had been dismissed. How they had crossed emotional barriers first, then sexual. He told of the time frame involved—more than a year in one instance. He went into as much detail as he believed necessary and appropriate, and when he finished his account, few questions remained.

The story was out in the open; no secrets. Ted shared with his congregation how the elders had met; how they planned to minister to the offending leaders; what the plan would be for caring for the innocent family members of the offenders; and how they, as a church body, would deal with this tragedy. This public disclosure was the first step in their plan for dealing with it.

"If you're feeling angry," he said to his stunned congregation, "it doesn't mean you're not graceful or loving. If you're not feeling anger, I wonder if you understand the hugeness of this!"

He spoke of his own feelings of schizophrenia—going back and forth between rage and confusion. And he stated the consequences of this sin in the lives of these three spiritual leaders: termination of ministry.

A leave of absence would not adequately communicate the seriousness of this situation. It could not be handled by "taking a break," he emphasized. But after explaining the consequences, Ted made clear the goal of the church for those caught in adultery: They would be restored.

Restored as people, and restored to the body, he said. Not restored to the staff—this was not the church's primary goal at that time. "The hallmark of this church is grace," Ted went on, "but consequences follow actions. And the task for the church is to hang on to these individuals, to uphold them as they go through the consequences. This event communicates the deadly seriousness of sin," the pastor told his parishioners. "Grace is our only hope, but grace does not remove consequences. Grace is not a soft mattress that cushions our fall. Grace puts shattered pieces together but does not prevent the crash that shatters."

Ted went on to tell the congregation that there

would be no secrets. That openness, as had always characterized this work, would be maintained.

Grieving the Loss

Later that same Sunday an afternoon forum was held for members who needed counseling. And on the upcoming Wednesday evening, all who needed comfort could meet with the staff and the elders.

Before the service ended that Sunday morning, Ted called all his elders to the altar. Then he said, "Some of you may feel so sad you just want to join us here and pray. Some may need to come and confess your own secret sin. Feel free to sit, stand, kneel, embrace one another, or come forward. Let the body minister to the body."

For a few moments, quiet settled over the congregation, and then a voice began to sing.

> We mourn, we mourn, O Lord
> for the price we pay,
> for the friendship so strained,
> for those families,
> for the trust that is gone.

The song was almost a wail, a melodic, minor key dirge. And with it came a great sense of release. As though an official period of mourning had been declared, the congregation grieved in unison, openly.

The rebuilding and repairing of damaged ministries would begin in time, but for now, the congregation's greatest need was the expression of its grief and all those emotions that are associated with loss.

Surviving and Going On to Effective Ministry

The approaches cited in this chapter were two different ways of dealing with a leader's sexual sin, and yet both resulted in healing. Of course, within each church were members who exited the closest door—offended, horrified, and repulsed—never to return. But hundreds more stayed, worked through their grief, and learned new lessons about grace and about the consequences of the sin against the body.

Not every church deals with the pain of losing a leader in an effective, healing manner—hence, the parking lot where a church used to stand; the handful of believers, a remnant of a congregation that once numbered nearly a thousand, meeting in a borrowed room. But of those that do survive and go on to effective ministry, certain characteristics are common.

1. *The sin was not covered up.* Whether in front of the congregation or in smaller groups, the sin was acknowledged openly. It was not denied by church leaders, nor was it excused or explained away. Also, the church did not try to shield itself from the scrutiny of the public/press. Its greatest concern was not its image in the community, but its own health and strength—both as a body and as individual members. Only when sin is revealed can it be dealt with—excised—so that the body can begin to heal and move toward strength and vitality.

In too many instances, church staff and lay leaders attempt to cover up the sin of a promiscuous leader, as if doing so will somehow protect the body from some terrible fate, as if the revelation of the leader's sin would be more harmful to the ministry than allowing him to continue. In reality, allowing a leader to continue living a double life eventually results in more harm to the body.

While the idea of making public a Christian leader's sexual sin is abhorrent, the alternative—allowing it to continue—is even worse. A church that is living a lie—whether deliberately due to a cover-up or out of ignorance—cannot be considered a healthy, successful church, regardless of the number of people sitting in its pews each Sunday morning.

Churches that survived the fall of their leaders know that this is true.

2. *The congregation was given opportunity to express its grief honestly.* In the churches where healing was accomplished, congregations worked to accept each others' emotional responses to the hurt and disappointment. For some it was easier than for others—some amount of censure is inevitable when strong feelings are loosed within a congregation. But the churches where members' feelings and responses were not controlled or manipulated fared better. The congregations faced the seriousness of sexual sin, perhaps for the first time. They passed through the various stages of grief that led finally to healing.

3. *Counseling was provided for church members.* In some churches, as in First Church, such counseling happened almost inadvertently as the body began ministering to itself. Mature leaders within departments and classes offered encouragement. Listening, they helped other members sort through their feelings and offered comfort and wise counsel. In other churches, counseling sessions were carefully planned and scheduled. In one prominent West

Coast church, professional counselors and psychologists were hired to work with the families directly injured by a leader's perversion. Each of these actions demonstrated to the congregation that the sin was regarded as serious, that its consequences were devastating, that the pain each member was feeling was valid, and that the harm done was deserving of repair.

Spiritual wounds are deep. Local churches that have found healing after the loss of a leader have been wise and attentive to the inner pain and confusion of their members. They have offered counseling and tried to minister to their people. They recognize that matters of the heart matter; that injured souls need more than a sermon.

4. *Plurality of leadership was in place.* A major factor among churches that survived the loss of a pastor to sexual sin was multiple leadership. Where there was a strong staff in place, churches were more likely to be able to maintain continuity as associate pastors provided direction and focus for the congregation. In those ministries dominated by one strong, charismatic leader, however, the church was more likely to fall apart after the discovery of his failure.

This was the case in the first church Andrea talked about as well as in Roger's church. In both of these situations, the pastor ran the ministry like a "one-man show," and when he went down it was very difficult for the show to go on. Plurality of leadership made recovery possible in most of the churches that survived the loss of a pastor to sexual sin.

5. *Recruitment of a new leader committed to strong Bible teaching followed the fall of the previous leader.* In

most instances, churches that have survived the devastation of a leader's moral failure have hired a new pastor who is a strong Bible teacher. As First Church's pulpit committee began the search for a new pastor, its desire for a strong Bible teacher was met with surprise within the denomination. For years, other churches had considered First Church a group that was not terribly concerned about careful exposition of doctrine and truth. First Church called its new pastor from a church recognized for its orthodoxy. He was a man whose first priority was preaching the truth, regardless of its popularity or compatibility with secular thinking. First Church, fed on truth, has grown strong again.

One church that nearly toppled to the ground after learning of its pastor's infidelity returned to its upright position soon after the arrival of a new leader known for unwavering commitment to the Bible. It is not uncommon, however, for less-mature pulpit committees to be attracted to a candidate whose knowledge of the Bible is secondary to his dynamic personality. In these situations, the committee seems inclined to believe that a vibrant, dynamic new leader will be able to pull a struggling, damaged work back to its feet simply by the strength of his personality and a series of "can do" sermons. But power in the *work* of God is inextricably linked to obedience to the *Word* of God, not to the personality or charisma of the preacher.

A fresh commitment to God's Word was an important step for many churches as they resumed their journey toward renewed spiritual power and joy. They took seriously Paul's instructions to Timothy, to "preach the Word . . . reprove, rebuke, exhort, with great patience and instruction" (2 Timothy 4:2).

6. *A plan of accountability was implemented.* In most of the churches that survive a leader's demise, accountability takes on greater importance. One church instituted a detailed plan for its leaders, requiring them to log their phone calls, all visitation in homes and hospitals, and any counseling sessions conducted at the office or elsewhere. Names of all individuals they speak with during the week are noted. The leaders meet together each week and examine one another's logs. Within this rigid framework, it is easy to note discrepancies. If on a pastor's log one name appears more often than any others, he may be questioned about it. Or, if he is seen often with an individual whose name is not on his log, it's likely he'll be asked about it. All this sounds very elaborate and, as one pastor told us, "If I have a mind to cheat on my wife, I'll find a way to cheat on this too." But it is a starting place, and it's important to remember that this church has been deeply hurt once and does not want to risk that kind of injury again. Its staff is willing to take these extra precautions to make it as difficult as possible for a leader to pursue a secret life.

Individual churches find their own best ways to create accountability, but one thing is sure: After a church has suffered the loss of one leader due to sexual misconduct, it does not want a repeat performance. Most churches want some sort of accountability system in place. The members are not so naive, not so trusting. They are more mature than before, and they want the freedom to question their leaders; they want them to be transparent; they want them to open their lives to scrutiny; they want them to know they are accountable to God, yes, but also to the congregation they serve.

Fragile Mud Dishes

The apostle Paul said of Christians that "we have this treasure in earthen vessels." In the aftermath of human failure, it is good to pause and contemplate the idea that we are little more than fragile mud dishes. All of us, whether leaders or laity, wear an ingredients label that reads: *Dust and divine spit.* And we wonder, how much can be expected from creatures made up of such unsavory components?

We study the sodden clay piled next to the potter's wheel and, shaking our heads, we say, "After all, it is only clay." But to the potter, it is the medium by which he will express his heart. He will plunge his hands into it, shape it, and turn it into a useful form. He will sign it with his name and give it value. He will guard it and protect it and use it with care.

Yes, we are earthen vessels. But the Potter dignified our existence by signing us with His own name and placing within us His priceless gifts. True, we are fragile. But the Potter who formed us is not helpless to protect us. He is omnipotent.

In the aftermath of sin, when hearts have been bruised and lives have been shattered, when we remember that we are little more than dust, it is good to also remember who our Potter is. It is good to remember that "He is able to keep us from falling."

11

Lives That Can Be Observed

Ah, the welcome respite of a Sunday afternoon. Church over, family fed, kids outside. For Kate the day of rest had just begun. She burrowed down into her favorite recliner, propped up her stockinged feet, and settled in with easy-listening music on one side, a mug of decaf on the other, and the weekend newspaper in her lap.

Kate pulled out the Sunday magazine and flipped through the pages. A blond from the cover caught her eye. The woman was being kissed on the cheek by one man while holding hands with another.

But it was the face of the man holding her hand—with his narrow smile, jutting chin, and sloped-nose—that riveted Kate's attention. For years that man had been her family's pastor!

Drawn to the text, Kate discovered that successful men willing to pay up to three thousand dollars could attend "Ken and Barbie" parties and meet beautiful women.

Kate stared in horror at the sickening picture of the man her family and her congregation had once considered their spiritual leader, a pastor who had left his church amid allegations of sexual misconduct. How could the man she had known as a teacher of the Word now be captive to the flesh? The wrapper looked the same but what had happened to the contents? The man, a once-visible representative of the spiritual realm, was now a tragic testimony of the carnal.

Gazing at the photo of her former pastor, Kate recalled her initial reaction to the news of his fall. Instinctively she had wanted to protect her children from any confusion and distrust that might threaten them spiritually. She knew she must be, in their lives, an example of Christian integrity, an example worthy of imitation. To herself she wrote a short note and assigned it to a corner of the bulletin board above her desk. The message reads: "Lord, let there be at least two people in this world that my children can respect as Christian examples—their father and me."

We Are Known by Our Deeds

None of us, *none* of us, relishes the idea of having our past scrutinized, our troublesome thoughts exposed, our weaknesses broadcast through bullhorns. We cringe at the thought of having our private lives put under the microscope.

Yet as Christians, what other testimony do we have but that of our lives? How else but by our deeds are we known? By our name? No. So much goes under the banner of "Christian" today that it's become more of an adjective than a definitive noun. By our words? Again no. Our actions either prove those words true or render them meaningless. Actions can make suspect even the clearest of spoken truths.

Like it or not, we are known by our deeds—and by the deeds of one another—whether good or evil. When one believer falls the collective church comes under criticism.

And sadly today, as one leader after another chooses to succumb to sexual sin, a revised "message" is being communicated to the world, a message which says: "Do what I say, but don't look too closely at the way I choose to live."

Then come the rationalizations.

The first few times we met it was to discuss problems in her marriage. As the pastor, I do all the counseling at our church, and for a while she made appointments to come to my office. But as our talks grew more personal neither of us felt comfortable meeting at the church anymore. Too many eyes in the walls. So we'd make dates for coffee, or I'd stop by her house when I knew she'd be alone. I don't know when our relationship changed, but there came a day when I held her as she cried, and I realized how much I deeply cared for her. We loved each other spiritually, then as friends, and then finally as lovers. There was a very natural, mature progression to our relationship.

It started at the funeral parlor, of all things. I had just lost my mother. And my pastor, a man whom I had known and respected for many years, stood by me, giving me support and speaking to people on my behalf. It seemed natural when he hugged me and put his arm around me and held me when I cried. I felt so alone; I needed to be held so badly. And then I remember him taking my head in his hands and kissing my forehead. He filled an emotional void in my life, and for months after that we had an affair. No one ever found out.

How easy it is to buy into a mind-set that gives us the right to usurp God's authority over our own lives and bodies; to forget that the God who created us has a right to tell us what to do; to forget that we were created to give glory to the Father.

Yes, we need to be loved. But during the times in our lives when we are either without a close companion or in a relationship that is emotionally unsatisfying, we still are loved. God has "loved us with an everlasting love." How then can we use the need for love as an excuse for immorality? How then can we choose to testify with our lives that God's love is insufficient, and that it is necessary to step outside His moral law to meet our needs?

Yes, we need intimacy. But during those times when we are without a mate or are experiencing emotional separation, God's grace is strong enough to meet that need apart from an immoral relationship.

Why then are so many Christians vulnerable to adultery and divorce? What rhetoric is competing with God's moral law, and winning? What liar is tempting us to take whatever pleases us and grab whatever promises fulfillment?

How Greatly We Are Influenced by the Social Norms of the Day

What is the one issue today most likely to push Christians to the point of taking a militaristic stance against popular opinion and controversial law? Probably most would agree it is abortion.

Think how the American mind-set on premarital sex has evolved in the past twenty years. In the fifties, it was a sin; in the seventies, a mistake; in the nineties, a right. (Pretty quick evolution.) And in the same period of time we have moved from *shame* as a deterrent to extramarital sex, to *abortion* as a quick fix.

Today the bottom line of moral decision making is the right to choose. Even the right to live must take a backseat to the highest of all rights: "What is best for myself." The argument used is "No one can tell me what to do with my own body."

We credit that line to abortion advocates, but aren't Christians saying the same thing when we rebel against God's moral law and choose sexual sin? Aren't we saying, "No one can tell me what to do with my body. I am responsible for my own happiness, and I answer to no one for my personal choices"?

Today if we criticize or even question a person's morality or ethics we are accused of intruding into their private lives. Our culture relegates God to the private sphere and tolerates believers only if they keep God to themselves. We're told, "Live your life the way you please, but don't force your narrow, conservative, antiquated ethics and morals on me."

This Privatization of God Is Dangerous in Two Ways

First, it labels all Christian influence as intrusive and suspect, narrow and oppressive. The world rightly recognizes morality's basis in God, but it rejects His unpleasant moral standards. This leads to the second danger. Realizing a need for some type of morality, people then define their own. And that definition becomes: "I am the center of all things."

How tragic when such thinking filters down into the Christian mind-set. When we too define morality in terms of *my* happiness, *my* fulfillment, *my* rights, *my* needs. I am the center; religion is peripheral. I am the vine; God is one of many branches.

Religion centers on *me*. No sacrifice. No heavy Bible exposition or sermons designed to make me squirm. Give me a three-step formula for meaningful relationships and a four-point motivational speech for building self-esteem. Religion no longer is about God; it's about my quality of life and how to get God to upgrade it.

Ministry focuses on *me*. I choose my church on the basis of programs offered. I'm drawn to church not because of who God is, but because of who I am and what my needs are.

Yes, it's good to help people who hurt, but if every time we come together the focus is on ourselves and our own needs, we may one day forget how to worship the Lord in the beauty of holiness, to sit awestruck in silence before Almighty God. We may forget that we are not the center of our own lives and that God is not the periphery.

The *Me* Factor

Ministry is about *me*. We've created "supply-side spirituality," writes Richard Ostling in *Time* magazine, "where God has become one of many avenues to success and self-fulfillment," and where our focus of faith has shifted "from the glorification of God to the gratification of man."[1]

---

[1] Richard Ostling, "The Church Search," *Time* (April 5, 1993), pp. 44–49.

Worship is about *me*. My needs satiate my prayers, and I expect from worship a sense of supernatural excitement. I present God with needs and I anticipate quick results. My prayers of adolescence haven't changed much over the years: "Just do this for me, God, and when I'm rich and famous I'll give you all the glory."

Relationships center on *me*. I am responsible for my own happiness, and if you're not meeting my needs, I'll find someone who can. If I'm not fulfilled in my present relationship, then it's time to move on. Life's too short to waste time being unhappy.

And finally, sin is defined and interpreted by *me*. If I have the ultimate right over my own body, if I best understand my needs and I consider them God-given, how easy it becomes to face down guilt and recriminations with a ready-made defense: "Private and personal; don't interfere."

Thus, in surprisingly few steps, we have positioned ourselves for a fall, no longer hearing about sin but instead contemplating our own personal rights and choices.

Getting Back to the Example of Christ

We seem to have forgotten that God understands our need for love and intimacy, and He will meet it, in His time, according to His purpose. He is Almighty God, and we can trust Him with our needs and obey Him with our wills.

We worship a God who took on human form and lived among us so that we could intimately know Him. He will meet our needs according to His purposes and carry out His plans in our lives for His glory. If we have anything to fear, it's our own propensity to focus only on the immediate and to seek to meet needs according to our own personal agendas.

If we choose to stand in defiance with the rest of the world screaming, "No one can tell me what to do with my body," if we substitute worship with self-gratification and theology with anthropology, we are then violating the very purpose of our creation.

It is only when I begin to understand who God is, when I am awestruck by His greatness and His majesty and His omnipotence, that I finally become humble, realizing that God our Creator does indeed have the right to tell me what to do with my body.

Each of us is called to be a testimony. We each carry the name of Christ and have in our lives those who look to us as their spiritual example, those whose faith would be vulnerable to Satan's attack in the event of our fall.

Paul's directive to "follow my example, as I follow the example of Christ" (1 Corinthians 11:1) at first seems slightly arrogant. Why even include himself as a middleman in this process? Why not simply say "Follow Christ," without offering his own life as a model and opening his own behavior to close scrutiny?

He did so because he loved the body and lived a life worthy of observation. Rather than shrink from scrutiny he welcomed it, inviting us to view his whole life as a testimony.

A call to moral purity is a call to establish lives that can be observed and to provide watchful eyes around us with an unobstructed view of our Lord Jesus Christ.

Vessels of Grace and Restoration

Sin as serious as adultery can't be fixed overnight, not due to a lack of love or forgiveness, but because sufficient time must pass in which that life, that moral character, can prove itself through the observations of others.

Christians, as one body, have an innate longing for oneness and wholeness and healing, whether twelve years go by, or twenty, or two. When our Lord prayed for us, He prayed that we would be one, just as He and the Father are one (John 17). But sin separates us, some sins more deeply than others, and restoration never comes easily.

As important as it is for the one who has fallen to reestablish a life worthy of examination, that same goal exists for the church. We as a collective body need to offer a testimony of God's loving healing and wholeness through the gentle restoration of the one who has fallen. Is it by our love, or our lack of it, that we are known in the world?

For those of us sensitive to a ministry of restoration within the body, there will be times when those we love will be hardened in their sin and will choose not to repent. In such cases, we suffer anguish over the loss of a spiritual relationship and face the heavy responsibility outlined in 1 Corinthians 5:9–11, which exhorts us to not associate with anyone who willfully continues in sin. We weep at those instructions and pray for the day when that person will repent and God will give him back to us. We learn to pray from a deeply broken heart. We experience the spiritual separation caused by sin, and we hate it. But in a sense it is a privilege to have this glimpse of the separation that turned a Father's face from His beloved Son at sin's fleeting moment of triumph. It is a privilege to share Christ's suffering and to know deep anguish over another's sin.

And if the suffering and the anguish is a privilege, think of the moment when the sinner acknowledges his sin and comes home. Think of the bond restored, of the body healed. Those of us who hurt due to the loss of a beloved brother or sister to sin's control should be praying daily for that phone call, that knock at the door, and that voice that says, "I'm back. I'm ready to heal. I need your help."

What a privilege to be a vessel of grace and restoration. To open our homes, to give honest guidance, to shield one from hurt, to give of our time and money and emotions, to laugh and weep. When he's hard on himself, we are God's gentle reminder of forgiveness. When she feels unloved, we are God's affirmation of love. When he's being left out, we walk alongside. When we hear rumors and gossip, we speak the truth in love.

We can welcome examination by the world if we acknowledge sin, confront honest anger and hurt and confusion, and end with a collective commitment to restore the fallen and a determination to not frustrate God's grace.

We have sought to extend in this book the message of joy and grace, and a call to moral purity through rightly labeling sin and guilt, acknowledging the pain of sin's consequences, and establishing lives worthy of observation.

When a leader falls and is restored, that life is then worthy of examination as a testimony of God's gracious love. "And the God of all grace, who called you to his eternal glory in Christ, after you have suffered a little while, will himself restore you and make you strong" (1 Peter 5:10).

All believers have at some time or other been broken. But no matter how bad our fall may be, no matter how many fragments we've been shattered into, we can still be pieced back together. And we marvel at the Craftsman who is able to lovingly fit each tiny chip back into place, and bind all those scattered fragments into a vessel of great beauty.

In these days when sin seems to have the upper hand, we need to commit ourselves to the strengthening and healing of the body, to continued warfare against sexual sin, and to establishing within our own lives living testimonies of God's love and grace that welcome observation.

God expects us to take care of one another.

Recommended Reading

Backus, William and Candace. *Untwisting Twisted Relationships*. Bethany House Publishers.
> A practical guide to restoring strong, intimate relationships by applying biblical truth.

Carder, Dave with Jaenicke, Duncan. *Torn Asunder: Recovering From Extramarital Affairs*. Moody.
> Strong on recovery, anger, and loss. A good text to wrestle with when it comes to laying blame.

Carter, Dr. Les. *The Prodigal Spouse: How to Survive Infidelity*. Thomas Nelson Publishers.
> Handles well the topics of deception, guilt, and restoring trust.

Colson, Charles and Vaughn, Ellen Santilli. *The Body: Being Light in Darkness*. Word.
> Absolute must reading—a lovely treatise on the unity of the body.

Conway, Sally and Jim. *When a Mate Wants Out: Secrets for Saving a Marriage*. Zondervan.
> Thumb through this first, but it does offer some good practical advice from this well-known and much respected husband/wife team.

Enroth, Ronald M. *Churches That Abuse*. Zondervan.
> Offers extreme cases of abusive churches, but is an interesting study of spiritual manipulation.

Fortune, Marie M. *Is Nothing Sacred?* San Francisco: Harper.
> An often-cited study of one church's experience with a pastor's sexual sin.

Johnson, David and VanVonderen, Jeff. *The Subtle Power of Spiritual Abuse: Recognizing and Escaping Spiritual Manipulation and*

False Spiritual Authority Within the Church. Bethany House Publishers.

> If you pick only one book to read from this list, make it this one. For those who have a hard time trusting religious systems, or who have been told that having an opinion shows a lack of submissiveness, or who, as Christians, have never been able to show on the outside what is happening on the inside, don't miss this book. We can't recommend it highly enough.

Laney, J. Carl. *A Guide to Church Discipline*. Bethany House Publishers.

> A thorough and sensitive discussion of this very difficult subject.

MacDonald, Gordon. *Rebuilding Your Broken World*. Oliver Nelson.

> A classic on restoration. Also a great place to test your "talking back" voice. While we greatly respect this writer, we encourage you to read this book with pen in hand, and talk through what's being said.

Pittman, Dr. Frank. *Private Lies: Infidelity and the Betrayal of Intimacy*. Norton.

> While this is a secular text, we strongly recommend it for its refreshing directness and clarity of thought, and for its treatment of the victim.

Rosberg, Dr. Gary. *Choosing to Love Again: Restoring Broken Relationships*. Focus on the Family.

> Excellent in its treatment of forgiveness.

Splinter, John P. *The Complete Divorce Recovery Handbook*. Zondervan.

> Strong on the practical.

Stafford, Tim. "The Sexual Christian," *Christianity Today*.

> Excellent study on the "Ethic of Intimacy."

Virkler, Henry A. *Broken Promises: Healing and Preventing Affairs in Christian Marriages*. Word.

> While there is much to talk back to and question in the beginning of this book, the second half is very helpful, particularly in its discussion of Genesis 3 and in its offering of specific lists of do's and don't's.

VanVonderen, Jeff. *Families Where Grace Is in Place*. Bethany House Publishers.

> A much-needed book on building grace-full marriages without legalism or manipulation.